REBOOTING...
LEADERSHIP

practical lessons for frontline leaders
(and their bosses) in the new world

MEREDITH
KIMBELL

RICHARD
HADDEN

BILL
CATLETTE

REBOOTING...
LEADERSHIP

practical lessons for frontline leaders
(and their bosses) in the new world

CornerStone Leadership Institute
P.O. Box 764087
Dallas, TX 75376
888.789.LEAD

Printed in the United States of America
ISBN: 978-0-9819242-7-4

Credits

Copy editor	Kathleen Green, Positively Proofed, Plano, TX info@positivelyproofed.com
Cover Design	Michael J. Hadden
Interior Layout	Melissa Monogue, Back Porch Creative, Plano, TX info@backporchcreative.com

Advance praise for *Rebooting Leadership*

"Just like coaches of successful sports teams, effective leaders must adjust their strategy once the game begins, in response to changes in the environment. *Rebooting Leadership* is full of useful tools for emerging and seasoned leaders in the constantly changing business world – tools that will improve their effectiveness and increase their level of personal satisfaction."

Adam C. Zylman, President & CEO, Sunland Capital LLC

"The Contented Cow legacy lives. *Rebooting* offers simple, solid, practical advice that is both timely and pertinent. It will be a 'must read' for my entire management team."

Brian T. Ennis, President & CEO, Etex Corporation

"*Rebooting Leadership* is a striking book, filled with wisdom and how-to strategies that leaders can use to build relationships, structure work, and get projects done more quickly and effectively."

Mark Levy, founder, Levy Innovation, and author,
Accidental Genius: Using Writing to Generate Your
Best Ideas, Insight, and Content

"*Rebooting Leadership* comes just in time. Frontline leaders face ever bigger roles and demands, but ever shrinking support for their success. These ideas are timely, practical and give them help they need."

Jane Altobelli, EVP and Chief People Officer, SymphonyIRI Group

"Too often frontline leaders are thrust into a leadership role with little or no training or coaching, adding a serious disadvantage to an already challenging assignment. The guidance and practical ideas outlined in *Rebooting Leadership* give them the information they need to be more successful in their roles."

Debbie Eshelman, Chief Operating Officer, SENSA Solutions

"Now, more than ever, frontline leaders need to be more engaging, agile and resilient. Their role is critical to company success. *Rebooting Leadership* will be a book they reach for when they want help meeting challenges that threaten to baffle, dishearten or overwhelm them."

Gary McKinney, Chief Human Resources Officer,
Valerus Compression Services

TABLE OF CONTENTS

1

IT'S A NEW WORLD

Reboot – *To reinitialize the execution of a program by repeating the initial program load (IPL) operation. Discarding much or even all previous continuity in the series ... to start anew.*

Anyone who has operated a computer for even a few hours is abundantly familiar with the process of rebooting – starting over. We reboot the computer when something throws its operating system into chaos, as that is the best (often the only) way to restore functionality.

In recent years, our *own* operating environment has been thrown into chaos as the result of near economic meltdown, financial shenanigans, wars, political strife, and, as Harvard professor Bill George puts it, "not subprime mortgages, but subprime leadership."

We're proposing that rebooting is precisely what we must do as leaders of communities, churches and, yes, businesses. We must put our leadership habits back on solid footing. With anything *but* new-fangled leadership, we must return to the fundamentals, the blocking and tackling, if you will. But, we must articulate and practice those fundamentals in a manner that reflects new realities. A world where folks are wrapped way too tight, trust is at its nadir, the deal in the workplace has been turned on its head, and speed is the key differentiator.

Think about it … If in 1999, at what may have been the zenith of American power, prosperity and prestige on the world stage, you had taken a long, 10-year nap, upon awakening, you simply could not connect the dots and rationalize the difference between the world you went to sleep in and the one you woke up in.

A lot has changed. In many respects we have learned to live with less security, less wealth, and to be less trusting perhaps of large organizations. On the other hand, we enjoy greater freedom of expression, less rigid career advancement, and access to virtually unlimited amounts of information. Moreover, for those drawn to jobs involving the exercise of leadership, we find that our roles are more visible and important than at any time in recent memory.

We have more impact, operate with less tolerance for error and, to be sure, at a much higher rate of speed than ever before. We're playing our game higher, faster, with greater visibility, and for more chips.

The decade of the 0's saw massive fractures of faith in business, government, even religious institutions. As a result, leadership has become more challenging, and yet for those brave and resolute enough to take on the task, it is at once both more relevant and rewarding.

Leadership – The Earned Consent of Followers

If nothing else, leadership is the earned consent of followers, consent that begins with the trust that, as leaders, we are who we say we are, and that even in the absence of guidelines, we will do what is right.

Throughout much of the first decade of the 21st century, the acts of a few rogue individuals and organizations had an outsized impact not just on financial markets, but the reputations of all those whose daily actions and decisions impact the lives of others. The implication for those of us who lead others is that we must re-earn that trust, and in a larger sense, re-qualify for duty. We must reboot. It doesn't matter whether we were approving bushels of shaky loans at Countrywide or diligently minding our p's and q's as an honest, hard-working floor manager at Claim Jumper Restaurants. We all bear the scars and the burden to reboot.

As Indra Nooyi, CEO of PepsiCo, put it, "Corporate America, after the immediate financial crisis, has now found itself thrown into a far more corrosive and durable crisis – a crisis of trust. The victims of recession may not differentiate between guilty and innocent parties – everyone in corporate America could take a share of the blame, deserved or not."[1]

> *"...everyone in corporate America could take a share of the blame, deserved or not."*
> INDRA NOOYI,
> CEO, PEPSICO

Followers Have Changed

The expectations and sensibilities of followers have changed, and by definition, so have their requirements of today's leaders. We no longer automatically enjoy the benefit of the doubt. There was a time when one's appointment to a position of leadership (at any level) came with the presumption that you knew what you were doing, had better than average insight, and could be counted on for a fair and rational thought process. No more.

In short, many people upon entering the ranks of management encounter a stiff headwind in the form of a "respect deficit" engendered not by their actions, but their job title. Let's just call it "guilt by pay grade."

So, too, the deal in the workplace has changed dramatically. People no longer look at their jobs through a long lens, "job" being defined as a sinewy, mutually beneficial relationship with a single organization. According to the U.S. Department of Labor, the average job tenure for working Americans has steadily decreased since 1950 from roughly 19 years to 4 years. As my* son put it recently, "I didn't marry this job, I'm just dating it."

Until recently when asked, "What do you do?" most people would reply, "I work at GM" or "I'm a nurse at Baptist Hospital," enunciating clear association with a particular organization. Now, more often than not, the reply is along the lines of, "I'm a systems engineer, investment banker, flight attendant" or something to that effect, with no tip of the cap to the organization. This came about not because we all woke up one day and said, "Hey, what I do is a lot more important than where I do it." Rather, the disconnect is due to a confluence of factors, not the least of which is the ongoing and often simultaneous bingeing and purging that occurs in most organizations today.

As a byproduct, many people have relegated themselves to permanent (or as permanent as anything is) free-agent status, rather than pursuing yet another "real job." Today, more than 10 percent of working Americans legally classify themselves as self-employed. For millions more, it's almost as if the payor entity named on the check is printed in disappearing ink.

Indeed, for many, it might be more appropriate to substitute the word "gig" instead of "job" to describe what we're about when we go to work, a word commonly used to describe the rather short-term appearances by a musician or band at a given location.

Untethered ... Sort of

Fewer of us report to the same physical address (except, perhaps for our home) when we go to work each day. For many, the work address is digital and it ends with ".com."

No longer tethered to a physical address, work for many has become boundaryless. Owing to a plethora of portable, often handheld wireless devices, we work from wherever, whenever. This is at times both a blessing and a curse. While it is liberating not to have our feet screwed to the floor in one place all day, those who fall victim to the device inevitably resent its intrusion into their personal space.

As a result, the deal in the workplace morphs a bit more as workers reason that, in exchange for the added intrusion into their lives, it is not unreasonable to bring personal tasks and interests into the work day and pursue them even when they're "on the clock." Indeed, author Richard Donkin's book, *The Future of Work*, makes clear the notion that, "Business must learn to share their people. Companies do not own the lives of their employees."

> *Business must learn to share their people.*

So What Does All This Mean for Managers?

For one thing, it means that you are now in charge of a workforce that is substantially and continually distracted by its newness; the constant change of owners, players, coaches, mission and priorities; and its relative inability to communicate beyond borders or even generations, not to mention distracted by all the constantly emoting e-devices.

It means, too, that your "position power" is diminished, in a host of ways. One of the traditional instruments of power, notably the ability to hold someone's job over their head, has lost its effect as each of us (outside of government, at least) have our jobs held over our heads every day. We've grown accustomed to it, and thus the threat has pretty much lost its impact. And, with the fluidity of people moving in and out of jobs/gigs on a regular basis, a manager's ability to institute long-term sanctions (e.g., disfavor, demotions) or, for that matter, rewards, is greatly reduced.

Not that you need to be reminded of it, but your job as a leader is less secure than ever, too. Not unlike what happens in professional team sports, when faced with an underperforming team, owners may be initially willing to trade a few players, but before very long, it is the coach who is in the gunsights. With practically no loyalty in play, the operative mindset is, "I can have a lot more impact by taking out that one guy than by trading players."

It's up to you to prepare yourself for duty (no longer will the organization absorb the lion's share of responsibility for your training/development). For one thing, the very first shoe to fall in a bad economy (either broad-based or company-specific) lands on the training budget ... every time. Moreover, as the deal in the workplace has become more transactional than it is relational, more things become a la carte. Not unlike the extra fees for checked luggage (tickets bought from a human, drinks, snacks or anything else on your favorite airline), your training is one of them. Trust us on this one, though. If you've got a boss or mentor who cares enough about you to candidly tell you where you need to develop/improve, and you have the maturity to really work at it, you're better off this way than if you had to wait for the organization's training priorities and resources to coincide with your needs.

It means you should expect the environment to be less collegial and more competitive as people rotate in and out. Bonds aren't as strong because they haven't been pressure tested by time and circumstances. And, there is a lot more self-interest in play; at some level we are all free agents. The good news is that self-interest is easier to spot – more visible than ever because it is hidden less and publicized more.

It means your learning curve is steeper. On one hand, you're expected to make mistakes, but on the other, there is less tolerance for error. When jobs were more of a "marriage" than a "date" as they are today, the learning curve was shaped like the flight path of a commercial airliner on a 1,000-mile flight, with a long, smooth climb to cruise altitude. Today, the entire flight may not last more than 300 miles, so the initial climb is shorter, steeper and bumpier. The honeymoon is practically nonexistent.

It means that there is no place for you to hide. In point of fact, with pressure from above and below, first- and second-level managers have *never* enjoyed much of a place to hide. Folks above you in the food chain have some ability to call a quick timeout, delegate difficult or unpleasant assignments, or, if things get really desperate, raise a lot of dust with changed priorities or a re-org, or throw someone else under the bus. Today, that is ever more the case. Just like on television, the "always on, 24/7 news cycle" is in play at work, too. Whereas it once took four or five months of bad reports for you to be in trouble and have your stock go down, now you can be drawn and quartered in 138 characters preceded by an "RT."

It means your opportunities to create a great team are better than ever. Old-school managers were expected to play the hand they were dealt over the course of a game that lasted much longer. Today, with less loyalty, more short-term assignments, a fluid workforce, and project teams that come together when needed, do their thing and disband, managers have much greater freedom of association. Moreover, with naked self-interest more at play, to include amongst your peers, it's much easier to stand out as one who truly values the interests, talents and opinions of others as much as your own. Thus, it's easier to become known as a talent magnet, and reap the rewards thereof.

It means that shaping your career requires more (and better) strategy. Vertical organic career growth (i.e., upward movement within the same organization) is diminished as there are fewer layers of management, many roles are farmed out, and Boomers just won't get out of the way. In that vein, it's more important for you to find the right *person* to work for than the right organization. That person, if so inclined, can take a more immediate interest in your learning and development, provide important growth opportunities, insulate you when you make a mistake, and share credit.

It means that you've got better developmental resources available to you now than ever. Today, an interested student can learn more online with a Google search and a Webinar, or an hour of self-study than they might have hoped to achieve in a two-day seminar 10 years ago. And, with another lesson borrowed from the world of sports, coaching is no longer a sign of social disease where D-players are sent in a last, desperate hope to be fixed. Today, there are more good coaches and mentors available, thus, they're more affordable. And, you benefit from the fact that technology greatly expands a coach's reach. No longer are you confined to working with someone in your same ZIP code. As a case in point, we probably hold as many executive coaching sessions online via video conference today as in person.

Today, managers waste far less of their time fighting and getting caught up in turf wars because there are fewer of them. Why? Because there are fewer "smokestacks" inside our organizations, and the ones that do exist are torn down more regularly. (Meanwhile, Millennials are wondering, what the heck is a smokestack?)

It also means that you've got greater real opportunity to contribute *and* to have your contributions noticed. Most organizations are very lean, and all hands on deck are fully occupied. Thus, you can seize opportunities to contribute if you spot them and are bold or brazen enough to take them on. Further, with the visibility induced by much flatter organizations, not to mention the digital opportunities to self-promote, your contributions (and shortcomings) are highlighted much more quickly.

This book is intended as a candid, practical assessment of how the touchpoints of leadership have changed, as many of the fundamentals remain constant, and how leadership will be practiced going forward, particularly by the women and men on the front line. And that is who this is for – the folks who work in the first couple of layers of management, those who might be contemplating the journey, and the ones responsible for their selection and coaching.

---

* Authors' note: Assuming the reader to be indifferent as to which one of the three of us is telling a particular story, or using an example, we have refrained from identifying ourselves individually throughout this book. Suffice it to say that no matter whose story it may be, we all three agree on the lesson drawn from it.

¹ *Fortune,* May 4, 2009

CHAPTER

2

BONE HONEST

None of us could live forever with an habitual truth teller,
but thank goodness none of us has to.
— MARK TWAIN

Referring to the 2008-09 global financial meltdown in the Oct. 3, 2008, issue of *Business Week*, Harvard professor and former Medtronic CEO Bill George noted that, "There is no doubt that failed leadership is at the heart of the crisis on Wall Street."[2] Had George expanded on his remark, he almost certainly would have attributed much of that leadership failure to people playing fast and loose with the truth. In some cases, this amounted to "lies of omission" as hundreds of people, for whatever reason, found themselves unable to approach decision makers with the truth. All the financial dust that had been temporarily spun into a pot of gold was inevitably going to disappear. In other cases, senior, "C-level" leaders told big, fat, bald-faced lies to their subordinates, investors, customers, and the general public about the dangers and impending implosion.

When you get down to it, there are lots, hundreds perhaps, of reasons for us to always do what our mamas taught us, and that is to tell the truth. Think about it. For openers, there really aren't any mysteries or secrets anymore. Any reasonably bright 15-year-old equipped with an iPhone, Google or Twitter can generally get at the truth in less than 10 minutes anyhow.

Another clear benefit is that your willingness to be candid (especially about yourself) causes others to reflexively be more candid with you. As a result, you will learn/grow faster and spend a lot less of your time sorting through BS. Indeed, this may be one of the greatest sources of competitive advantage available to you. And, people tend to have much greater respect for those who level with them, particularly when those folks are in a leadership role.

The problem is that truth is like a knife with a very sharp blade. Used well, it can raise levels of performance, teamwork and innovation. Used ineffectively, it often results in someone getting hurt, perhaps you, as many a whistle-blower will agree.

Sadly, as a result, too many people, including some in leadership positions, are unwilling to summon the courage to take definitive positions on *any* matter. Lynn Harris, a Montreal-based organization development specialist, has written an excellent piece on the subject on linkageinc.com in which she suggests that our reasons for avoiding truth-telling "boil down to three basic causes, Socialization, Fear, and Skills."[3] On the premise that we can't do much about the first of these reasons, we'll concentrate on the latter two.

Wife to husband: "Does this new green dress make me look big?" Spouses and significant others often (and with good reason) run for the hills when they hear a question like this. Truth be known, the only safe answer at that moment is "no," even if it shades the truth. Even pretending you didn't *hear* the question is dangerous. It is a very slippery slope, indeed.

Telling the truth is at once a matter of caring and a matter of responsibility. If you care about people, you tell them the truth.

Every bit as importantly, you make it possible for them to do the same with you. On an important matter, blowing smoke up someone's skirt (or green dress) may be flattering for

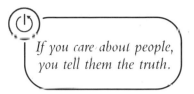

If you care about people, you tell them the truth.

a short while, but it is one of the unkindest things you can do to them. As a case in point, I have personally witnessed hundreds, no, thousands (yes) of people terminated from their jobs for poor work performance after having been told formally (verbally and in writing) that they were doing a good job.

> *Forget outside competition when your own worst enemy*
> *is the way you communicate with one another internally.*
> — JACK WELCH

So, what is a frontline leader's obligation as it pertains to truth-telling? Is it any different from the obligation that non-leaders have for doing the same?

Second question first: Yes. Your obligation as a leader to be truthful is considerably greater than that of the average person. Why? Because you're expecting other people to follow you, sometimes on a difficult journey. They're not going to do it for long if you prove to be unreliable or unacquainted with reality. George W. Bush lost the benefit of the doubt with people the world over when he obfuscated the reasons for going to war in Iraq, declared "Mission Accomplished" too early, and then felt compelled to continue redefining the mission and stated reasons for being there.

Now, to the matter of a frontline leader's obligations vis-à-vis the truth:

1. **Recognize failure and call it what it is.** Frontline managers get the chance to swing at a lot of pitches. You hire and un-hire people; make daily decisions about production or workflow matters; you allocate, schedule and procure

resources; arbitrate or otherwise resolve disputes, and the list goes on. In short, you get a lot of chances to get stuff wrong. And unlike those who are senior to you, you're not afforded the luxury of calling timeout, deferring or delegating a lot of these chances.

You're going to make your share of mistakes. When you do, step up quickly and say so. Don't wait to be prodded or bludgeoned into doing it. Learn from your mistakes, but don't torment yourself. If your mistake has caused harm to others, make it right as best you can. Move on.

During the Major League Baseball season of 2010, umpire Jim Joyce made a bad call, one that cost Detroit Tigers pitcher Armando Galarraga a perfect game. As there have only been about 20 perfect games in MLB history (as of this writing), this was a big deal.

Galarraga's reaction was calm and professional. And, apart from the error, Joyce demonstrated why he has long been considered one of baseball's finest umpires. Immediately after the game, he reviewed the video, publicly admitted his error, and sought out Galarraga to apologize. My guess is he didn't wait to consult his lawyer, league officials or game sponsors.

Occasionally you're going to drop a ball or make a bad call. When you do, like Jim Joyce, own it and speak up … quickly. When others do the same – and have confidence that they won't be bayoneted on their error – they too can move on, and everybody can get some work done.

Perhaps my greatest failing as a young, Level 1 manager was in being so focused on avoiding mistakes that I failed to swing at some really good pitches. In retrospect, I missed out on some really good opportunities because of it.

2. **In discussing unpleasant matters, don't hide behind policies, cultures or others.** Both space shuttle in-flight accidents that resulted in fatalities (Challenger and Columbia) are linked (in one case directly attributed) to people not speaking up when they had solid reason to believe that a serious problem existed. In each case, a culture rooted in a rigid caste system overran the courage required to speak up.

   Our best advice for you in this area is predicated on the belief that you get paid to think, to think critically, and when necessary, to let your voice be heard. If an important point (let alone one that involves a matter of life) is not being made, it is your job to speak up to an appropriate audience. Do it calmly, rationally and in a thoughtful manner, but do it.

   Chronically waiting for others to get their oars in the water or silently deferring to others is chicken; it's cowardice. And, it's no longer an option. Just ask the families of the dozens of soldiers who died on Nov. 5, 2009, at Fort Hood, Texas, at the hands of a fellow soldier whose disturbing history was known and ignored.

3. **Speak truth to power.** If your boss is about to "step in it" (or is already knee-deep), needs to know it, and will permit your candor, tell her. Go to her directly – privately and forthrightly. Then, forget that the conversation took place. As organizations continue to flatten, it's inevitable that you'll find yourself having more dealings with people who are senior to you. Often, they will ask for your input on something. This is a perfect opportunity for you to develop a reputation as a well-informed, non BS'ing, tactful truth-teller. Some tactical advice follows:

Do	Don't
Voice what *you* have seen, heard, know, or believe.	Speak for others or pre-suppose what they might think.
Do your homework – be informed.	BS, or be afraid to say, "I don't know, but I will find out."
Offer your opinion as factually and tactfully as possible.	Ramble, spin or try to game the situation.
Speak about issues and concerns.	Personalize your criticisms.

If your boss won't tolerate candor, find a new one, soon!

4. **Critique like a coach.** As a frontline leader, you are more a coach than anything else. You're not the team owner, a star player or the general manager. You're a *coach* who is supposed to guide and direct others to an objective and help them perform better. As such, appraise others' performance regularly and fairly and candidly … always. Undervaluing performance (or failing to recognize it at all) takes the wind out of people's sails; overvaluing it can cause them to stop short of their full potential.

If you attend stage performances in the U.S. with any regularity, you may have observed that most shows, unless they're really awful, receive a standing ovation, deserved or not. After a really standout performance, the standing O is often spontaneous and unanimous. Other times, a few enthusiastic supporters stand, followed by many others who seem to just be following the crowd. They may be feeding the players' egos, but I doubt they're doing much for the actors' development.

I recently saw Rodgers and Hammerstein's *Oklahoma!* performed by a professional touring company in Glasgow,

Scotland, where I think audiences may be a bit more judicious in their appraisals. The show was excellent – pure entertainment! But it wasn't quite standing-ovation material. The audience applauded enthusiastically, but from a seated position. The message to the cast? Great job. Step it up a notch, and you'll bring the house to its feet.

When we give everyone a "5," "Outstanding," or "Consistently Exceeds Expectations," we leave no room for those who truly are at the top of their game. We do no favors when we tell someone they've reached the summit when the summit is actually just a few yards away. As a frontline leader/coach, remember that not every performance deserves a standing ovation.

> *Not every performance deserves a standing ovation.*

5. **Keep it balanced.** Build support for the truth by acknowledging your own culpability. If your team's productivity fell last month, be the first to face your productivity issues and explore your contribution to the shortfalls of the team. When people see that you aren't simply using the truth when it is convenient to your point of view, they immediately become less defensive.

6. **Make it easy for others to tell you the truth, or at least what they think.** In his book, *Who's Got Your Back*, author Ken Ferrazzi points out that if you get angry, argumentative or push back when getting feedback, the other person will make a mental note to self, "I won't be doing this again." He encourages us to think of feedback as impersonal data to be combined with other information and then run through our decision-making wheelhouse for possible new action.

7. **Practice.** Practice (that's right) having difficult conversations with peers, mentors and others with whom you have a comfortable relationship. By observing their reactions and listening to their feedback, you can more clearly define the "edges" of the playing field and make more effective choices of how to play.

Managers in a service company we know stopped telling the truth after several employees reacted to unfavorable feedback by complaining to a senior manager who then reversed or deleted it. Even harder, when it came time for employees to give leadership feedback, the frontline managers faced comments commonly called "drive-by shootings" that stayed in their files and impacted their raises. With some guidance and practice on giving effective feedback, they could have avoided this pain as well as the pain of trying to achieve tough goals with mediocre team players who never improved.

If people are going to follow you, they have a right to know where you stand. And "stand" means stand.

We're not trying to turn you into a Don Quixote and have you tilting at windmills by blurting the truth at every conceivable opportunity. Nor are we suggesting that you adopt the supposed courtroom standard of telling "the whole truth and nothing but the truth." But, if people are going to follow you, they have a right to know where you stand. And "stand" means stand.

It's also important to make another distinction. People whose quest for "truth" becomes dogmatic have been known to be more dangerous than those who can't even *spell* the word. That's how women in some cultures wind up oppressed and without opportunities for education. That said, bear in mind that your reputation as a leader is the biggest thing you've got going for you as a leader. Your reputation is founded in no small part on whether or not people find you to be a straight shooter, even when (no, *especially when*) it is unpleasant or unpopular.

Yet, too often in our modern world, it is a technique of last resort. Only when we are forced up against the wall with evidence that is undeniable do we, often embarrassingly, admit to the truth.
— DAN STRUTZEL

Monday Morning 8 a.m.

In this and every succeeding chapter, we've included a section we call "Monday Morning 8 a.m." – clear, executable prescriptions to help you with rebooting leadership. We suggest you tackle one chapter's worth of these "doable things" at the beginning of each workweek, before you get bogged down with the necessary, the important, the urgent, and the mundane. Here's the first set of prescriptions:

1. The unvarnished truth makes such rare appearances that it can be off-putting to people. Try counteracting that by first seeking permission to be candid, e.g., "May I be completely candid with you?"

2. Starting today, do a self-audit periodically to ensure that you are being as painstaking in highlighting people's strengths as candidly and as often as you do their weaknesses.

3. Identify one person on your team who can be counted on to regularly tell you the truth (things you need to know but may not want to hear) and thank them.

---

[2] *Business Week*, Oct. 3, 2008

[3] "Truth-Telling: Confronting the reality of the lack of candor inside organizations," Lynn Harris, Linkage, 2006-2008

CHAPTER

3

REBUILDING TRUST

In researching this book, we surveyed more than 400 managers and professionals from diverse organizations and levels. Survey respondents told us unequivocally that the most important component of leadership in today's world is trust. No other factor even came close. Why? Trust is the key that unlocks the highest levels of innovation and performance, which are essential to speed of execution. Without it, everyone operates at best deliberately, at worst protectively, and in either case, slowly.

Sadly, the economic crisis pushed what had been a basic orientation of trust in business and financial systems right past skepticism into a deep mood of cynicism.

> *Without trust, everyone operates at best deliberately, at worst protectively, and in either case, slowly.*

Even if, as individuals, we hold zero responsibility for creating that cynicism, we must still address it in order to engage the effort, creativity and productivity needed to succeed. More challenging yet, we must discover how to build others' trust and loyalty in the face of greater distances, speed and chronic changes.

Julio Olalla of the Newfield Network observes that, in every culture, high trust builds under the following conditions:

1. **Competence:** You wouldn't trust your car to an incompetent mechanic.

2. **Sincerity:** You wouldn't trust your money with a banker who promised one rate of return in public, then unilaterally changed the agreement to something lower.

3. **Reliability:** Would you subscribe to a newspaper if the carrier missed your house one day each week?

4. **Capacity:** You wouldn't hire a moving company with one truck and one driver to relocate the contents of an 80,000-square-foot office building.

Fundamentally, trust describes a person's willingness to risk. When you employ others, or accept them onto your team, you risk their willingness to show up as required, contribute their effort, and behave responsibly. In return, they risk their time, effort and spirit with you. It's up to each party to maintain and strengthen that willingness. Here are four ways you can do your part:

Start Strong

If you are lucky, when you find yourself in a new position or starting fresh with a new team, you'll find people willing to work with you to make the transition a smooth one. In reality, that doesn't always occur. As a leader, remember it is your party and *you* hold the responsibility for welcoming others, not vice versa.

Many times you will step into situations with a difficult history and face:

+ An exhausted, broken or low-performing team
+ Team members with leftover "attitude" from previous gigs, or your predecessor
+ People skeptical of working for someone of a different age, gender, ethnicity, or style

+ Free agents who bring diverse expectations of you and their work

Other times, you will start fresh with a team that doesn't know one another, or you.

In every situation, be the first to reach out to team members. They want to know who you are, where you're going, and what you're made of. If you are silent or act coldly toward others, they will tend to believe their fears rather than your hopes. Before you've said too much about yourself, though, demonstrate genuine interest in *them* by asking about their aspirations, strengths, preferences, and how you can help them succeed. Here are some additional tips that have helped leaders at all levels:

+ Share a big (but credible) vision for the future. Realistically describe compelling outcomes for them and your team. Share your hopes and expectations for participation and contribution.

+ Demonstrate by your actions that you are worthy of others' trust. Act with competence, sincerity and reliability.

+ Be quick to call out any behavior that erodes trust, asking for new solutions and agreements to correct it. When trust has been irreparably broken, deal with it swiftly and surgically.

+ Ask others to tell you when something you do erodes their confidence and support. Make sincere efforts to change, and tell them when you can't (or won't) change.

+ Bake trustworthiness into your hiring, recognition and retention processes in a big way. Never ignore, excuse or sanction breaches of trust.

Build Strong Self-Trust

Insecure leaders leak their uncertainty in many ways ... all damaging. Being hesitant, unclear or indecisive certainly doesn't draw people to you or inspire them to give you their best work.

As a leader, you're expected to stretch the edges of capability for everyone on the team, yourself included. You pursue ambitious goals and explore unknown territory, dealing all the while with the imperfections of others, knowing they will surprise and frustrate you at times. You can't escape mistakes, yours or theirs.

Your self-trust can suffer badly, but without it, you won't be a fully capable leader. With strong self-trust, you can stay clear, fair, thoughtful, and productive with less stress.

Steve sometimes felt like a 10-year-old leading a team of eight. Rather than lead, he withdrew and worked at his desk doing the familiar responsibilities of his old job. He avoided giving clear directions so others would like him, but then felt angry and threatened when anyone expressed frustration about not understanding his expectations. Rather than show what he feared was weakness, he attacked them for not thinking on their own. Instead of building anyone's effectiveness, his lack of self-trust eroded everyone's confidence and motivation.

A few tips for fueling trust in yourself:

Do	Don't
Make only agreements you fully intend to keep. Control your priority list.	Be afraid to say "no." Overcommit yourself or your team.
Keep your sense of perspective and a learner's attitude. Appreciate the fact that you are human, and move forward.	Take setbacks as the end of your biography, not just the latest chapter in your story.
Call on friends and trusted advisors. Debrief and ask for their support.	Isolate yourself. Work without guidance from experienced leaders.

Do	Don't
Find lessons and share your teachable moments with others. Become a more valuable coach.	Discount your role in mistakes. Blame others. Move on without learning or teaching anything.
Forgive yourself as fast as possible.	Doubt, chastise, worry endlessly.

We've had an extraordinary year, despite major inflation of raw materials, and I can say that the single biggest contributor has been an increase in trust. We now move through enormously complex decisions at breakneck speed.[4]
– AL CAREY, CEO, FRITO-LAY

Rebuilding Trust When Relationships Break Down

As the pace and complexity of the game increase, we tend to become less reliable. Hence, there is a greater tendency to unintentionally disappoint, undermine and frustrate others. Policies and technology won't change this, so when you fall short, it is up to you to clean up your messes well.

Think about a time when you talked with a skillful customer-service representative after being frustrated by a lousy product or service. If they handled it well, you came away not only relieved, but trusting the company more and telling friends about your "amazing experience."

Several years ago it happened to me. I had a terrible experience with an L.L. Bean rain suit that caused me to be cold and wet for better than 24 hours. The service rep was so good at expressing regret on behalf of her company and trying to make me happy that I wound up buying a more expensive rain suit from them. More importantly, I've continued to buy more stuff and sing their praises ever since!

A few tips for how to rebuild trust:

Do	Don't
Face the music. Step up and say when you've dropped the ball or negatively impacted others. Be the model for how you want others to clean up their messes.	Pretend the mistake didn't happen. Ignore or minimize it. Believe others won't notice.
Say how your mistake happened and what you'll do to avoid recurrence.	Make people wonder if you "get" what happened, its impact, and what you must do differently.
Empathize, apologize and fix any issues you caused others. Make them whole as best you can.	Ignore the extra work, time, resources, and waste you cost others.
Ask for forgiveness and the opportunity to re-earn their trust.	Believe others will forget. Assume your regret alone is sufficient to restore others' confidence in you.
If a relationship is completely irreconcilable, let it go and move on. Control what you can, your own attitude, and your ability to start fresh.	Think you can repair every mistake. If others won't trust you again, try to force them. Wait to move on until they support you.

When Another Has Broken Your Trust, How Do You Rebuild It?

Just as you don't intend to cause breakdowns with others, they seldom intend to hurt you or your team. Few people come to work looking forward to doing a bad job, but it happens.

If a breakdown happens, the cause is clear, and you know the other person will fix the problem, sometimes a smile and some encouragement is perfect. Other times, addressing the problem will take more effort.

Janet published a document under her own name when Bill had actually written it. In another case, Sarah talked with Andrew to ensure they agreed on the presentation for the leadership team, but in the meeting, Andrew went rogue and argued a different view that left Sarah looking ill-prepared.

While handling broken trust isn't fun, it is essential for building high-performance relationships and results. Sometimes raw anger is

> *While handling broken trust isn't fun, it is essential for building high-performance relationships and results.*

important to express, but, to resolve a breakdown, you must move beyond it. Anger can interfere with learning what happened and making new agreements for the future.

If you are committed to rebuilding broken trust, these next tips offer guidance that can help:

Do	Don't
Address shortfalls only after you've "counted to 10." You can't be constructive when you feel destructive.	Ignore mistakes that matter. Increase stress and suspicion by simply swallowing and moving on.
Recap any broken agreements and name the shortfalls. Check that you both perceive the situation in the same way.	Address issues before there is mutual understanding of agreements and shortfalls.
Ask what happened. Readily admit your own shortcomings. Ask others to reflect on their mistakes in ways that help them learn.	Tell them why they failed, or lash out. Use leading questions, e.g., "Don't you think …?" that only ask them to agree with your positions.
Look to the future. Ask for and make new agreements, "Going forward, will you … ?" Ask for any repayment or help you believe is appropriate.	"Play with dead snakes." (In other words, don't keep replaying the past.)

Building trust and repairing it skillfully when it's broken is a continuous task of highly effective leaders at all levels. Gaining trust requires your sincere commitment, skill and time, but it is one of your most powerful strategies for leveraging the loyalty, collaboration and creativity that your organization needs to thrive in the new economy.

Monday Morning 8 a.m.

1. Do an inventory of anything you are thinking or doing that erodes your self-trust. Talk with a good friend or coach if you need help creating the list and defining ways to improve. Begin today ... what are you waiting for?

2. Revisit any recent mistakes you've made that have caused others heartburn. Clean them up in ways that rebuild others' respect, hope and willingness to follow you.

3. Assess whether you are avoiding others or perhaps failing to expect their best because you've lost faith in them. Define what changes you'll ask them to make that will rebuild your trust, and then talk with them. Explain what you want and why. Honor them by re-engaging them in being more successful.

⁴ *The Wall Street Journal*, Sept. 20, 2009

CHAPTER

4

RIDING THE WAVES

Any surfer knows to expect good days and bad. Some waves exhilarate you with the ride of a lifetime, while others leave you disoriented and gasping for air under tons of rushing seawater. As a leader, like the surfer, you've signed up for rigorous duty with chills, spills and occasional thrills. In either avocation, you *will* get sand in your pants.

In your career you will experience some great wins, fantastic people to work with, loyal customers who want more of your work, and opportunities to build something you're immensely proud of. On the flipside, bad times will occasionally blindside you, and like a punch in the gut, take the wind out of more than just your sails. They come when:

✦ You are impossibly short staffed and resourced but still expected to deliver great results

✦ The project you've invested so much in delivering loses funding or is taken over by someone else

✦ Others claim credit for your work

✦ Your company makes a terrible mistake that harms you or people you care about

✦ You miss important family events because you simply can't get away

They can flatten you. Moreover, as the pace of change quickens, challenging times will increase in frequency and severity. While you can work to avoid the bad times, at some level they are inevitable. The question becomes, "How can you face setbacks so you are most ready to catch (and ride) the next wave of opportunity?"

Prepare for Great Opportunities

Surfers don't spend 100 percent of their time riding great waves. Much of their time is spent swimming to get out past the break line (preparing), then sitting astride their boards looking seaward to spot and choose their next rides (scoping). You would be wise to do the same.

Preparing for opportunities means staying in shape physically, intellectually, financially and emotionally so you have the capacity to handle new challenges. A C-level coaching client recently showed up for our 7 a.m. meeting fresh from the gym, where she had already completed her workout. It struck me that, if she thought it important to make preparation her first priority of the day, I should probably consider it, too.

Preparing means investing in you and your team's development so that, individually and collectively, you are ready to take on bigger stretch assignments. If you are ready and your team is equipped to succeed (with or without you at the helm), it's easier for others to choose you for the next big opportunity.

*Whether as a surfer or leader, you **will** get sand in your pants.*

Finally, preparing means exercising your creativity and adaptability muscles. Choose assignments (even hobbies) that stretch your thinking and style. One leader we know studies jazz singing to stretch her versatility in style and presentation. Another, a Baby Boomer, takes computer lessons from the twenty-something "geniuses" at an Apple store in order to stay relevant. Another listens to TED regularly to gain exposure to coming trends and ideas. Whatever interests and nourishes your creativity and perspective, invest in it.

Keep your network extended and vital so that when new opportunities appear, you are among the first to know. Then, as you do with your e-mail inbox, decide which ones are worth exploring. Surfers anticipate about every seventh wave being a bigger, more interesting challenge. If they (or you) choose to ride only little waves, you'll get too comfortable and achieve the same ol' results. Learn to gracefully decline requests that don't optimize your contributions and energy. Learn to wait, spot the juicy waves, and swim fast to catch them.

Stay at Your Best

When trouble hits, would you rather meet it feeling anxious, discouraged and doubting your ability to survive, *or* resourceful and confident? It's a no-brainer, but too many leaders go immediately into a state of shock, neglect their opportunity to make choices in a critical moment, and thus prolong the hard times. The early handling of the 2010 BP Gulf oil spill comes immediately to mind.

So, how do you find your most resourceful, best self? Before your next crisis (as in now), write down a description of how you show up when you are at your best. What do you think about yourself, your talents and your ability to find your way through any challenge? Write those beliefs down starting with "I ..." e.g., "I love challenges ... I am creative and know how to find the resources I need ... I can inspire people to help." What are three of your most self-empowering beliefs when you are at the top of your game? Write them down.

_____

_____

_____

Vividly recall a specific time when you faced a challenge and were at your best. Right now, let your physical posture and breathing shift to match how you were then. Do you sit up straighter? Breathe deeper? Smile? Feel tingling in your chest or deep calm and focus? Describe how you show up physically when at your best.

_____

_____

_____

Once you identify your most resourceful beliefs and posture, practice them every day on your way to work. When you face a big opportunity or a daunting challenge, it is often hard to remember, much less "find" this state of advanced readiness. The more regularly and vividly you practice re-experiencing your "best self," the easier it will be to call it forward when you need it most. The outside world won't change, but your inside ability to handle it will improve dramatically. (Besides, it will give people next to you in traffic something to wonder about.)

Valuable Lessons From Surfers

When surfers get disoriented underwater after being dumped by a big wave, they can't immediately tell up from down. They re-orient by relaxing during the initial uncontrollable period of turbulence. Then, as it passes, they exhale slowly to watch which way their air bubbles go ... that is "up." They follow the bubbles to air and a fresh start. The practices below will help you find "up" and a new start at work.

Learn to Relax, Deeply

When a setback hits, learn to relax long enough to get your bearings. Unless a situation truly demands instantaneous response, there really is value in "counting to 10." You can calm your system enough to access your best responses, not knee-jerk reactions you might regret later.

Survival experts maintain that people die unnecessarily because when they panic, they fixate on the threat (e.g., fire, attacker), thus completely overlooking opportunities to escape. Those who widen their field of vision and search for options survive far more often. They may not actually count to 10, but they intentionally override panic with an exhale and will themselves to a calmer state. It helps them see opportunities, not just obstacles.

Remember the Bigger Picture

There is a world beyond any threat or loss you face. When caught in a monster wave, it is easy for new surfers to believe that experience is *all* of reality. Experienced surfers know that both thrilling and crushing waves roll through. With a broader perspective, they operate resourcefully, assured that a new ride is in their future. Or, as Grandma used to say, they know that "This too shall pass."

Eric was a frontline leader whose team so angered a big client that they took their business elsewhere. He'd endured angry meetings and long nights to rescue the situation. He did everything he could, but it wasn't enough. Like a teenager experiencing his first major love loss, Eric felt like his whole world had crashed. He couldn't see any future and even considered resigning. Granted, losing a love, a client, or getting swallowed in a nasty wave is not fun, but with time and experience surviving a few of these situations, your bigger picture helps you recover faster and sustain your courage and optimism when you need them most.

Remind yourself of other times you've survived setbacks and disappointments or conquered fears. What beliefs and practices helped you most? Replay the mental DVD containing those experiences and use it to ready yourself for what lies ahead. Many top athletes and other performers listen to a favorite song to prepare themselves for a big performance.

Avoid the temptation of going on a distracting "I-deserve-it" binge. Eating, drinking, shopping, etc., don't really help you and can have painful consequences. Addictions have been defined as "never getting enough of what you don't need." When crushed, define what will truly nourish your spirit and help you move forward. Find it and give *that* to yourself instead.

Remember What Is Most Important to You

One of the most powerful ways to expand your perspective and re-orient effectively is to reconnect with your Core Commitments (the values and purpose that mean most to you in life).

To shift metaphors for a moment, anyone who's watched a triathlon knows that trailing well behind the leaders is an amazing group of physically challenged athletes who compete with the aid of prostheses and modified bikes. These people have chosen to act on their Core Commitments rather than succumb to a victim mentality. Not unlike our friend Eric Weihenmayer, a blind, world-class mountaineer, they are quick to let you know that whereas they may be disadvantaged, they are not disabled.

Many leaders become great leaders because they've endured and learned powerful lessons from horrible life experiences. While some people collapse from these situations, leaders find their way and come through them stronger, wiser and more inspiring to others. How? Core Commitments are a big part of the answer.

A commitment is a choice. Your Core Commitments are choices so central to your being that you never release them. Physically challenged athletes have discovered their passion for competing and making the most of opportunities, whatever it takes. Parents have discovered they will sacrifice their lives for their children. Leaders who identify and then persistently act on their Core Commitments tend to stay creative, resilient, engaging, and more successful over time.

The I-beam

Imagine that someone has securely placed a steel I-beam on the curb, spanning the width of a city street. The beam is but 7 inches off the ground, all traffic has been stopped, and someone offers you $1,000 to walk across the beam to the other corner. Would you do it? Of course. What if the beam was raised to a height of 10 feet off the ground, and now they offer you $20,000 to walk across it? Some would no doubt consider it. Finally, the beam is moved to a height of 290 feet, spanning a narrow, 80-foot-wide canyon in southwestern Colorado. Heavy winds blow up and down the canyon all day long. Would you walk across it, say for the same $20,000? For $50,000? Probably not.

How about if the person offering you the money dangled your young child, or someone dear to you over the edge and threatened to drop them? Would you walk across the I-beam to save them? You bet. Think about, and make a list of the things in your life that you would be willing to walk the I-beam for. These are your Core Commitments.

> *Make a list of the things you would be willing to walk the I-beam for. These are your Core Commitments.*

Another way is to think how you most want people to remember you when you are gone. What experience do you want them to have of working and living with you? What would you love to know they said at your funeral or wrote on your tombstone?

A third option is to think about what totally fulfills you about leading. What actually happened on those days when you climbed into bed and said, "That was a great day"? Why? What values and purpose did you express or what did you accomplish that meant so much to you?

_____

_____

_____

What are three of your Core Commitments? Don't worry if they don't seem like typical business words.

_____

_____

_____

Now that you've gone to the trouble of identifying these commitments, if you're really serious about living your life by them, tell three people who will hold your feet to the fire. Later, when you find yourself stuck, disoriented or momentarily knocked on your keister, take time to reflect and then act from your Core Commitments. They will guide effective choices that leave you fulfilled and encourage those around you.

Use Your Lifelines
Never swim alone, especially in rough water.

Successful leaders establish strong lifelines to people they trust. People who will make time for them, tell them the truth, help them in tough situations, mentor them, open doors, or just take them out to dinner and listen when there is nothing to do but share the comfort of a friend. They view these people as a personal "board of directors."

Who is on *your* board? Who do you turn to in a crunch? Not sure? Then start looking, now. Who is a model of the leader you aspire to be? Ask them to mentor you, being mindful and respectful of the time commitment. Who do you trust to give you bone-honest feedback and advice? Let them know you value the relationship and ask if they will help. Who will listen compassionately and keep an airtight confidence? Treasure them. Respect their time.

If you know your lifelines, write them down, now. Have you ever noticed how hard it is to think of even one person to call when things are really tough? If you write down your list, it will help you think clearly and make good choices when you most need the help.

_____

_____

_____

Remember to thank your lifelines richly and reciprocate their generosity. If you can't return it, "pay it forward" to those who need your assistance.

When You Hit the Rocks

Ann got fired. Frank was unjustly accused of sexual harassment. Ian's team was pulled into a frivolous lawsuit that cost a year of his time and career advancement. There are setbacks that really hurt, some permanently. How do you recover?

In addition to the ideas above, there is another way we seldom discuss in business: Forgiveness.

New leaders often feel righteous indignation about others. "That was bad, wrong, and should never have happened. How could they! They deserve punishment. I'll show them, at least with my attitude."

Or, some criticize themselves, "I am pond scum. There is no hope for me, ever." While everyone gets angry at times, successful leaders visit vengeful thoughts but leave them as quickly as possible.

When heartbreaking things happen, do you let your heart scar shut and vow never to risk again? If so, you are constricting your life. If you let heartbreaking things break your heart open instead of shut, you will gain compassion, tolerance, courage, and eventually, greater capacity for participating in life's abundant opportunities.

Breaking "open" to new possibilities requires forgiveness, of yourself and others. It requires a clear-eyed acceptance that no one is perfect. Even the "good guys" screw up and do things that leave them ashamed, humiliated and remorseful. You'll meet a few people without a conscience who really do mean to hurt you, but you can stay by choice. You can let them close you or open you. The path to opening includes forgiving.

Think of forgiving as a selfish act, one that frees you from investing any further energy, effort, sleepless nights, and aching stomachs over bad experiences and people you no longer trust. Forgiving doesn't mean you forget, or approve. It does mean acknowledging that keeping your Core Commitments requires you to choose to stop investing energy and attention in the people and situations that will divert and cripple the future you want to create.

Helping Your Team Recover

This chapter has centered on personal recovery, when something happens to *you*. But when shocks happen to your *team*, how fast can you re-engage them? Your answer is an important assessment of your leadership skills.

First, focus yourself. Let go of any nostalgic longing for the past. It's gone. Focus on what you can change: the future.

Think clearly:

+ What's the new situation? What is most important to understand and face?

+ What are the most powerful, valuable places to focus given the new world?

+ What can you and your team contribute that adds big value?

+ Who and what can you leverage to get a jumpstart on success?

You don't need all the details, but for a strong start, know the basics.

Once you have a plan, do the following to mobilize key players:

+ Name what is at risk if they don't change and adapt — make the picture hit them viscerally. Mobilize their concern.

+ Present a compelling picture of what they can create for people they care about a lot — clients, the company, their teammates and themselves. Define what differences they can make that *they* value. Mobilize their caring.

+ Give them the first few steps for getting started so they know what actions will help create a positive future. You can ask for their ideas, but take the initiative to point to clear first steps yourself. Mobilize right action.

+ Increase hope. Remind them of their strengths, previous success, your confidence in them, and any available resources. Mobilize courage.

+ Set a date to follow up.

Learn what will help key contributors get back on their feet fast. A comforting ear? An "Irish Wake" to celebrate the end of the old so they can let it pass and get on with creating the future? A tough-love challenge to step up and give their best? New skills development?

Everyone wants to work with the "comeback kid." Be the leader who won't give up, and who is resilient and creative enough to rise and succeed again. Influence others to act like comeback kids, too. Make adaptability a core value, competence and source of pride on your team.

So What?

Surfers don't learn to surf by reading about it. They master surfing by practicing regularly and loving the practice, on good days and bad. Enjoy and be nourished by inspiring times, and remember to navigate the challenges you face like a surfer. This is the path to becoming the consistently successful leader others want to follow. Which surfing skills will help you succeed most?

Monday Morning 8 a.m.

1. List the names and contact information of people you want as your lifeline relationships. Make a date to meet with one or two of them soon so you start cultivating their readiness to help long term. Ask for advice on something that you'd like to learn, e.g., networking, hiring, leading, navigating politics. Ask for their guidance on handling a challenge. If you discover they are willing to help, express appreciation for their assistance and ask for permission to talk with them again. Find out how you can support them and deliver. Make your lifelines reciprocal.

2. Write down your beliefs, attitudes and physical characteristics when operating at your best, and practice using them several times a day. Practice when you get ready for work, on your commute, and before meetings.

3. As you hit opportunities and challenges today, ride them like a surfer.

CHAPTER

5

GETTING STICKY

No man is an island...
— JOHN DONNE

Getting what?! Getting sticky. Marketers work to make their ideas sticky. They want people to associate with them, remember them, take action on them and come back for more. That sounds a lot like what leaders want, too. We create stickiness when we engage with people, organizations or ideas in ways that generate attraction. We do it by creating common vision and purpose, sharing sacrifice, and acting in ways others find trustworthy. We create bonds that last until either natural or managed forces break the adherence. But, it's not easy.

Where the *position* of leadership used to be sticky in and of itself, that is no longer the case. Today, leaders must make *themselves* and their *agendas* attractive in ways that make people want to engage with them. And this, as employment expectations, obligations, terms of engagement, and the very nature of the work have all changed significantly. Some of the more stark changes they must address in the new world include:

✦ **Mobility** – Most of us are no longer chained to a desk, a shift, building, department, job, project, manager, cost center, or even an employer, to the degree we were a few short years ago.

✦ **Stability** – Budgets and priorities change in mid-period. Our leaders move in and out of positions often before we get to know them, or they us. Team compositions change, without notice or explanation. Peers, friends and customers are all "reassigned" willy-nilly. We spend months building a relationship with someone who up and leaves without clearing it with us. The nerve! Clients hire, fire and re-hire us; and the projects we're working on get moved up, down and off the hot list with dizzying frequency.

✦ **Connectedness** – Perhaps due to the aforementioned mobility, while we're electronically *over*-connected in many ways, most workers are far *less* connected to people, places, schedules, and work (as in *outcomes*) than their predecessors.

What has not changed at all is our need for connectedness and the experience of belonging. Psychologist Abraham Maslow positioned social needs, including the need for belonging, smack in the middle of his famous Hierarchy of Needs, ahead of esteem and self-actualization, and just behind protection from physical threat.

Opening the Kimono

Consider Facebook. Its success is rooted in the fact that people desperately want to get beyond the transactional nature of their existence and have others take a greater interest in them as individuals. Why else would you risk the not insignificant downsides by putting all your pictures, secrets and daily goings-on out there for the world to see?

The workforce you lead is likely a mélange of scheduled and unscheduled employees, contractors and those who regard themselves as lifelong free agents. If we are to truly enroll them or "get them sticky," we must demonstrate that same interest in the people on our team. Even those whose paycheck comes from Payroll (rather than A/P) are likely to see the relationship with their current employer as but one stop on an itinerant career path. The whole point is to get your ticket punched, add marketable skills, score some cash, get benefits coverage for awhile, and move on. No emotion, no strings attached.

Today's lack of connection results in several (mostly unintended, and unwanted) consequences:

+ Because we don't *really* know them, we act on uninformed assumptions about some of the people we work with. We may never even have *met* them. We do the best we can with the information we have.

+ We find it difficult to match talent and desires with work assignments.

+ Individual development needs are frequently ignored.

+ When it comes to rewards and recognition, we often (no, *usually*) get it wrong. Because we don't know enough about what each person values as a reward, we opt for the generic. Everyone gets a gold star, whether they appreciate gold stars or not.

+ People lose touch with the meaningfulness of their work.

+ Communication loses effectiveness, and often, efficiency. The better you know someone, the more you can rely on a common language, code, shorthand, even a knowing glance across a crowded conference table.

4.1 years

Four point one years. That's the average job tenure for U.S. workers, reported in 2008 by the U.S. Department of Labor's Bureau of Labor Statistics.[5]

When one's "term" in a given job is around four years, workers can become like elected officials, distracted from day one by the need to create the next opportunity. Stickiness – or connectedness between worker and organization – is marginal, and may be lopsided. A 2009 poll published in *USA Today* showed that a bare majority (57 percent) of employees considered themselves "loyal" to their employer. But, get this, only 25 percent of the respondents felt that their loyalty was reciprocated.[6]

> *When one's "term" in a given job is around four years, workers can become like elected officials, distracted from day one by the need to create the next opportunity.*

The need to connect remains strong, however, and so, in many cases, employees shift their connection from the organization … to the work itself, to individual leaders, or to some non-work-related aspect of their lives.

Classical management theory suggests that managers exist chiefly to do four things: Plan, Organize, Direct, and Control. This collection of necessary and insufficient skills even had its own acronym: PODC.

While the most effective managers throughout history were also concurrently good *leaders of people*, the role of leadership didn't garner much attention until the 1950s. Since then, heroic leaders – both well-known and to a greater extent, those heralded in our own minds and hearts as people we'd "walk through fire for" – have been those who knew not only how to PODC, but also how to inspire people to produce more value through their discretionary effort.

Technology has frequently found a welcoming home in the workplace, ostensibly to make our work easier. But, there's a dark side. It's probably more accurate to say that, in many cases, technology has also made our work more voluminous. The fact that we *can* now track every production, service and cost variable to the nth degree doesn't mean we should, but many persist anyhow. But clearly, our use of technology, along with organizationally induced distance (remoteness), has diminished something without which no workplace can function: trust.

As a social being, we tend not to trust those we've never laid eyes on to the same extent as those with whom we've broken bread, or at least a few coffee mugs. We likely never will. As a result, we've got to put real effort into getting to know people, *really* know them, one at a time. We need to take an interest in them, listen to them better. A *lot* better.

Pre-Millennial leaders learned, mostly by observation and example, how to lead, influence and build relationships based on a model rooted in personal contact. Training was done in a classroom where if the instructor sneezed, you might catch her cold. Meetings were held in a time and place certain, and all attendees were actually contained within the same four walls. Legendary negotiations were carried out in the infamous "smoke-filled room," with all the parties hammering it out face to face, Marlboros ablaze. Yes, much has changed.

Today, technology, often originating in someone's kitchen or garage, has taken over nearly all of the old but still necessary functions represented by PODC. But technology alone is profoundly inadequate. Commercial airline pilots control the takeoff and landing of their aircraft with admirable skill, but much of the rest of the trip proceeds cybernetically. Witness the unintentional "flyover" of the Minneapolis/St. Paul airport by two experienced, but – for more than an hour – *dis*connected (and later, unemployed) Northwest Airlines pilots on Oct. 21, 2009. Amazon.com's phenomenal inventory management system knows, as if by magic, precisely when to order stock, so as to simultaneously maximize the needs and interests of such diverse constituencies as their suppliers, customers, and their cash register.

So what's left, you ask, for us mere mortals to do?

What's left is to lead, connect the players and dots, and create stickiness.

It seems safe to say that our mastery of technology will fall short of a reliable and effective application for leading and influencing others to create and sustain value.

Casting the Show

As a manager, one of your *most* important jobs (maybe *the* most important) is to decide who gets to do the work your team is tasked with doing. In a well-worn but nonetheless effective model, you'd go out and look for someone who could do the job, interview likely suspects, and hire the best of the lot. Whatever "best" means.

Today you're as likely to arrange with someone to do a job without offering (burdening?) them with a traditional employment relationship. Legions of self-employed graphics artists, programmers and nurses, downsized from their corporate employers, do the same work, for more money, and a much greater variety of clientele, than they did when they held a "real job." They've traded the illusion of stability and group health insurance for freedom, more direct control of their time, and the terror of being their own boss.

Our first company logo was designed in 1997 by a bearded, geeky creative type who worked in a graphics design studio housed in a funky office space not far from mine. Eleven years later, our new logo came from logotournament.com. We went online, described what we wanted, how much we were willing to pay, and put the job out for competitive bids. More than 30 designs were submitted, from every corner of the globe. The winner was a Spanish artist with a lowercase pseudonym. I've never even been to Spain.

Code writers, medical transcriptionists, nurses, even C-level execs freelance their labor to the buyer offering the best deal. But the connection to their "employer" is at arm's length, insulated by layers of disconnectedness that can't *help* but manifest themselves in ways both small and large. Heard in the break room: "Are we supposed to invite David (a contractor) to the Christmas party?" Heard in the management meeting: "It's Ellen's (a temp) birthday — do we need to get her a cake?"

Irrespective of the ultimate legal nature of the relationship, you've still to determine who (as in what human being) will produce the best results, for the best investment. As we've said emphatically in our previous books, the best hiring outcomes result from careful attention to the matter of "fit." Does the person (traditional employee or free agent) have the potential to be happy, productive and successful working for (in, around, with — you pick the preposition) your outfit?

The answer to this question matters … a lot. And if the answer is "no," you owe it to all concerned to carry the relationship no further, regardless of how talented the person may be.

And if *you* are being held accountable for results (and you *will* be, one way or another), your only hope of picking the best person for the job lies in knowing, *really* knowing the person you're extending the offer to.

Automated recruiting and selection has become big business. If your applicant volume is big enough, your company probably uses it. We get the allure of such systems. Sifting through hundreds of apps for a single position could surely benefit from some electronic intervention to separate the wheat from the chaff. It's inevitable, though, and too bad, that lots of wheat is blowing off with the chaff, and too much chaff is getting hired as wheat.

As sophisticated as some of the best of these systems have become, no one has yet to build one that adequately replaces the act of sitting down with an applicant, eyeball to eyeball, to engage in the process of assessing the likelihood that that person's coming to work for your organization – on whatever basis – is best for them, and for you. In fact, given the loosey-goosey nature of the resulting employment relationship today, this is more important than ever.

Had the producers of *Britain's Got Talent* relegated their recruiting and selection process to an automated system, Susan Boyle would likely still be known only to a relative few, including a cat named Pebbles.

e's and r's

Terry Brock is a relationship marketing and technology expert. His clients and friends automatically associate him with all things geeky. I run into him a couple of times a year, and each time, he's attached to some amazing new gadget that I end up reading about months later in a technology column. But, as Terry told me via a video Skype call while he was visiting Panama, it's not about the electronics; it's about relationships. "Everybody goes on about e-commerce, e-this and e-that," Terry said. "But in spite of all the 'e's,' it's really the 'r's' that matter. We ought to be talking more about 'relationship-commerce,' relationship development, and how we get things done through the relationships we've worked hard to build. The electronics are just a vehicle, a tool – and don't get me wrong, they're pretty cool vehicles, and I *love* using technology – but when the power goes out, the batteries are dead, the satellites are down, and the dog chewed through the cable, we still need our relationships to get anything done."

> Nugget: Technology is good. Relationships are important. Neither is a good substitute for the other.

Indeed, talking with Terry, with crystal-clear clarity, while seeing his face and expressions (for free!) made my interview with him better. But had I not spent time with him over the years, visited his home, had meals with him, and shared an audience with him, I would have just been some guy writing a book. The electrons have certainly facilitated, but the relationship's foundation is personal. And it also has to be that way with the people you lead.

Getting to Know You

As established above, leadership requires, above all else, a personal connection with those who would follow. It involves a level of engagement and participation on the leader's part that cannot be delegated to another person, or to a system, process or machine. Leadership is personal. If you don't treat it that way, you're going to have a nearly impossible time attracting and retaining great followers.

Here's an incomplete list of things, most of which you need to know about each person you want to make sticky:

- ✦ Their name. You think we're being facetious. We're not.
- ✦ What they're really good at, at work and elsewhere.
- ✦ What they do for fun, at work and elsewhere (up to a point).
- ✦ What they are lousy at.
- ✦ What they'd like to do better.
- ✦ Their strongest passions (what they stick to).
- ✦ How they get to work each day, how long it takes, and what they go through to get there.
- ✦ Their most powerful life experiences, good and bad, which color their approach.
- ✦ Who (and/or what) is most important to them, outside of work. Don't pry, but open your eyes and ears. If they don't want you to know anything about their personal life, that's a choice you should honor. Otherwise, tune in about their spouse or partner, their kids, grandkids, parents, and pets. Know when something significant is going on with these people, when they're seriously sick or hurt, and when they accomplish something worthy of congratulation.

✦ How they're particularly suited to serve some need at work. Example: They spent a year mentoring kids in a country where one of your customers is from. Would that connection help your customer, and the employee?

✦ What they're having trouble with … and could use your help with.

Thanks, Boss, I Look Forward to Meeting You Someday

Someone came up to me after I'd spoken at a convention and asked how they could be effective as a leader of people they've never even met. Not wanting to discourage them, while remaining true to my opinion, I said, "Unless you're way better than any other leader I've ever heard of, you probably can't. Certainly not with core team members." You simply can't provide the same richness of support and leadership at a geographic distance as you can when you at least occasionally occupy the same space. And let's not forget, if your employee has never met you, or rarely if ever spends any meaningful time in your presence, they can't possibly know best what moves *you*, what impresses *you*, and how best to support and follow you.

At the very least, we've got to acknowledge that lots of people are visual learners. You can read their resume, talk to them 'til the cows come home, and e-mail them incessantly, but they're not buying in until they can get belly to belly with you, or at least look you in the eye.

Breathing the same air is best, but not always possible, or affordable. This is where technology makes a valuable contribution. Connect regularly by videoconference, Skype, or other visual VOIP providers. Communicate better and more frequently with a remote team by developing an ongoing series of podcasts. Anyone can do it. You don't need a sound studio, background music or anything elaborate. Do the podcast, give them access, and they'll stick it in their ear. And that's a good thing. The technology to do all of this is getting more accessible all the time, so access it.

In a practical sense, increasing face time is really a matter of creating, and seizing upon, opportunities to get together. Some ideas:

+ Plan, and budget for, *at least* one dedicated opportunity per year to get together with everyone on your team, no matter where they're located. Be smart about it. Determine if it makes more sense for you to go to them, or vice versa. Meet them *en masse*, one at a time or in clusters, whatever's most doable. But stop talking about it, quit making excuses, and do it.

+ Take advantage of coincidence. Pay attention to travel schedules. Don't ever waste an opportunity to drop in on a team member, or extend an invitation, whenever your respective travels (business or personal) put you in the same area code.

+ Attend the same conferences or training events, and schedule time – at least a few hours, if not a whole day – on either side of the event, to get in each others' faces … constructively.

And I'm Doing This ... Why?

Finally, people can't possibly do their very best work if they don't fully understand why their work matters – what ultimately becomes of the tasks they perform, the ideas they implement, and the relationships they develop. The more mobile, transient and loosely connected we are to the people we co-labor with, and the entities we work "for," the more intentional we have to be about shining a bright light on the purpose of our daily work, and the end customer.

> *People can't possibly do their very best work if they don't fully understand why their work matters.*

To do that:

+ Create (as in contrive, manufacture, demand) opportunities for people at every stage of the value chain to see how customers ultimately derive usefulness from their work. Go on field trips, share customer testimonials, illustrate to people how the job they did last month has made somebody's life better.

✦ Facilitate communication between groups within your organization. Let the folks in Indianapolis know how their work helped the group in Brussels, how Engineering impacts Sales' success, what happens when (and only when) Supply Chain is attentive to details, how Collections fuels the ability of R&D to probe new technologies, and the list goes on.

✦ During the regular one-on-one conversations you have (you *are* having them, aren't you?), ask people to tell you how their work intersects with the organization's mission. (Hint: Make sure they have a clear sense of your mission first.)

Monday Morning, 8 a.m.

1. Spend 15 minutes looking for the "low-hanging fruit" about how you can create and strengthen the relationships with people on your team.

2. Schedule an in-person 1-on-1 with a core team member you haven't been in the same room with for a long time.

3. Identify a constituent, customer, or support group with whom you need to strengthen the relationship, and schedule an appointment to visit them.

4. Rate your personal and/or departmental relationship with each key business partner, client, supplier, or interface on a red-yellow-green scale. Schedule lunch this week with someone on the "yellow" list.

---

5 U.S. Dept. of Labor Bureau of Labor Statistics, Employee Tenure Summary, Sept. 26, 2008

6 *USA Today*, (Randstadt/Harris Interactive "Unrequited Love" Nov. 11, 2009)

CHAPTER

6

YOU GET PAID TO THINK!

You are today where your thoughts have brought you;
you will be tomorrow where your thoughts take you.
— JAMES ALLEN

"You get paid to think!" The line rolls emphatically from the lips of actor John Houseman in the wonderful, classic training film, "Brain Power," based on Karl Albrecht's book of the same title. Houseman takes the audience through a series of exercises designed, in part, to help us think, and perhaps in larger part, to demonstrate just how little thinking most of us actually do.

If Albrecht's message had application in 1980, consider how much more useful it is today, as:

+ Work is more complex, interrelated and driven by the need for speed. As a result, we often find ourselves in "mess management" mode, rather than thoughtful problem solving.

+ Massive volumes of information (electronic and otherwise) are constantly inbound over the transom, all vying for a share of our "brain space."

+ The majority of people now entering the workforce have

been steeped in a team culture. Much good has come from that, but it does affect the way we think. Groupthink … 'er GroupGrope. From kindergarten to college, today's new workers have been schooled in teams, they've heard their parents talk of team initiatives at work, and now they're organized into "teams," often very transient teams, in their own jobs. In these organization forms, *someone's* thinking, but not necessarily everyone. Indeed, teams can be a good place for non-thinkers to hide.

✦ We've consolidated the jobs of many into just one, eliminating redundancy and overlap. As a result, we have to think more – much more – about priorities, interactions and outcomes.

✦ Throughout the developed world, brain work has substantially overtaken brawn work.

In short, a higher order of thinking is required today, and most of us aren't prepared for it. Indeed, the near meltdown of our financial system in 2008–2009 was precipitated in part by a bunch of extremely smart people who weren't thinking very clearly. It was if they had suspended rational thought and resumed believing in the tooth fairy.

Incentive systems and a fixation on quarterly earnings reports have conditioned us to focus on short-term (*very* short-term) results, to the exclusion of activities (like thinking) with more strategic consequences. While we do, in fact, get paid to think, it *looks* like we get paid to optimize quarterly earnings. Indeed, the prevalence of sophisticated metrics, dashboards and feedback mechanisms is sufficiently seductive as to make us shun thinking in favor of relying on numbers, which inevitably flow out the other end of those tools. We become like the pilot who is totally consumed by his flight instruments, to the exclusion of what is going on outside the aircraft.

One of the casualties of this movement away from thinking has been the development of thinking skills and making space for thought in the course of a manager's day. Learning to think, practicing, making mistakes and having successes are a huge part of professional development. But without circumstances that compel us to think, to make hard decisions, and to make the inevitable mistakes, we rarely do. The result is poor decisions or no decision at all, which in itself is a decision (and usually the wrong one).

Mirroring what takes place in our nation's schools, we have witnessed a pervasive movement in business toward scripting the responses, phrases and actions of workers at all levels, to include managers, rather than encouraging and expecting people to think for themselves.

Rules of *Disengagement*

The autumn of 2009, while not great for leaf colors in North America, did bring a stunning display of mindless application of rules in both the public and private sectors. Delaware first-grader Zachary Christie was nearly suspended from school for 45 days for innocently bringing a Boy Scout camping tool to class, in violation of his school's zero-tolerance weapons policy. Loud community protests caused the district's administrators to *think* for a change about the absurdity of the punishment, and the decision was reversed.

The manager of a St. Louis Burger King expelled Kaylin Frederich and her mom from his store because Kaylin wasn't wearing shoes. She was six months old and carried in her mother's arms! And, 25 students at Perspectives Charter Middle School in Chicago were arrested, taken to jail and booked for engaging in a food fight in the cafeteria. These high-performing kids from an inner-city college prep school now have criminal records because they tossed their cookies *before* eating them. It's hard to imagine that anyone thought through the sensibility of this while summoning the police.

In the U.S., thoughtful political discourse has become increasingly rare as both major parties have further polarized to the right and the left. Everything's either black or white. Red or blue. Since we don't have (take) time to think through the issues, we just lean to the side that feels more comfortable at first blush. Besides, why should we do our own thinking when we've got MSNBC and Fox News to do it for us?

This aversion to thinking extends to the workplace. We've got so *much* to do, in so little time, that thinking gets shorted. It's easier to clump people who share certain characteristics into branded groups than it is to think about them individually. We apply rules and policies with reckless abandon, never thinking about how the rule helps or hurts the business. And, perhaps worst of all, we fail to think through issues, stopping to consider what's different across them. As a result, we apply familiar solutions to fresh problems and wonder later why the patch didn't hold.

> *We apply familiar solutions to fresh problems and wonder why the patch didn't hold.*

For our part, we have actively resisted, at our own peril, client requests to package leadership techniques into a handy, idiot-proof mantra of scripted catchphrases and acronyms so that managers could get through the day without overheating too many brain cells. Witness all the "performance review in a box" products that currently exist.

> *The sign of a first-rate intelligence is the ability to hold two opposing ideas in the mind at the same time and still retain the ability to function.*
> – F. Scott Fitzgerald

Remain Situationally Aware

In the course of their jobs, pilots, soldiers, surgeons, and power-plant operators (among others) consider not only the current data, but the environment, their experience and intuition to assess the current situation and extrapolate the projected outcome of their decisions. Failure to remain situationally aware has been identified as one of the primary factors in accidents attributed to human error. When you encounter a situation that *appears* new, ask, for starters, "What else is this like? Where did it come from? How does it impact my team?" Similarly, when you encounter something (or someone) that *seems* familiar, resist, at least momentarily, the urge to label and classify.

Beware Data Waterboarding

It's hard to get anything done, let alone think, when you spend the majority of the day with your lips wrapped around an information fire hose, a condition we refer to as "Data Waterboarding." Indeed, various sources have suggested that e-mail volume alone has now reached a level of 100 billion messages per day worldwide, the vast majority of which are irrelevant and unwanted.

Having more information than you could ever possibly use, right at your fingertips, is both a blessing and a curse. The blessing is that, in the decade of the 1's, there simply aren't many secrets anymore. If you really want to find something out, you can do so quickly and relatively inexpensively. The downside? The very second you toggle the data switch into the open position or venture

> *It's hard to get anything done, let alone think, with your lips wrapped around an information fire hose.*

near an open Web portal, you experience the digital equivalent of what radio host Erich "Mancow" Muller felt when he volunteered to be waterboarded in his unsuccessful effort to prove that waterboarding didn't constitute torture.

Managers, most of whom no longer have the benefit of administrative support, experience this at some level every day, dealing with scores of data impulses that come to them in digital, paper, telephonic, and human form, and many days it indeed feels like torture. "When will I have time to do *my* work?" And just like what occurs everywhere else, a lot of this is spam, too. If you're part of a larger organization, the "switch" gets toggled for you as others both inside and outside the organization have virtually limitless ability to dump things into your inbox (snorkel), and dump they do. Clearly, it's not all stuff that you need or want.

To show how far we've come (notice I didn't say "progressed"), my parents' generation considered it very bad form not to examine and then respond personally to each and every incoming phone call or piece of written correspondence. In fact, my dad was annoyed whenever he heard that I had rail dumped an entire batch of e-mail forwards from some of his friends. Clearly, for the better part of three decades, we've been moving at a velocity and with volumes of input that make that totally unthinkable. So don't try. Here's what you *can* do, though …

Get ruthless. Realize that, not unlike the function performed by a medical triage manager, you *must* sort through this stuff and become proficient at separating the vital (the ones that have stopped breathing) from the merely urgent (slow bleeders) and the folks who are merely seeking attention. Fail to do this, or do it poorly, and you will drown. And, consistent with good triage, be clear that a lot of your inbound, a majority perhaps, doesn't need to be opened or dealt with at all, ever!

> *A lot of your inbound communication, the majority perhaps, doesn't need to be opened or dealt with at all, ever!*

Triage, as practiced today in every modern hospital emergency department, derives from the French term *triagere*, meaning "to sort." The concept was first used by Napoleon's battlefield surgeon, Baron Dominique Jean Larry, who deduced that having some process by which to rationally allocate limited medial resources to the needs of incoming casualties would yield better outcomes.

Triaging seems highly applicable to the process of optimizing data flow to the modern manager as it involves rapid assessment of need (relevance and quality of data in our case) and rationing of care (time and attention). As a manager, you must constantly bear in mind that, while data are useful to doing your job, they are not the job itself. Moreover, in most cases, having too much data is as debilitating as not having enough. No, it's worse.

Gen. Colin Powell, a truly exemplary leader in many ways, has long subscribed to a decision-making theory whereby, in the heat of battle, the optimum practical point to make a decision is when you have about 60 percent of the available information, *and* you've expended no more than 60 percent of the available time. That's the point at which you've likely got sufficient data to make a reasoned decision and can still take advantage of being an early mover. Gen. Powell's advice is helpful for another reason, as well. It reinforces the value of having not just the right amount of information, but getting it at the right time. Stale data are about as useful as stale bread.

Use "mission relevance" as one of your primary means of ruling information either "in" or "out" of your field of attention. If you are a floor manager at a casual themed restaurant and your store's mission is to survive a tough economic period by maintaining and even improving guest satisfaction, incoming data about the opportunities to buy properties vacated by a failed competitor aren't especially helpful to you. For one thing, that information is probably better suited to someone in a different department and pay grade. Moreover, it really doesn't pertain to your mission.

Though you can (and must) use an industrial-strength spam filter to keep other types of "unit growth" junk out of your datastream, it is even more important to train your eyes to scan arriving messages, regardless of their source, for "mission relevance." The ones that seem relevant deserve a quick read before further sorting into an appropriate "bin."

For your peers and direct reports, (and even your boss), teach them to identify their issue, the action they want from you and how urgently they need your response in the subject line of their e-mails. "Big Client at risk needs your decision by 5 p.m. today" is a valuable subject line. Likewise, provide the same clarity in your e-mails to them. When you send information to others, format reports so they can quickly see what is truly important. How many reports do you complete that don't seem relevant, clear or streamlined, i.e., waste your time and fall into a black hole?

While scanning your "pile," make note of whether you are a primary or secondary (cc'd) addressee. In the case of the former, the likelihood of your needing to at least read the item is substantially greater than if you've merely been cc'd along with a hundred other folks. Of course, if the sender is north of you in the food chain, it might be a good idea to read it, regardless. If nothing else, you can check to see if they spelled your name correctly.

Be a librarian. Just as a librarian certainly doesn't know what's in all the books, you needn't attempt to have recall or understanding of all the stuff that lands on your pile every day. But, if you're a good librarian or a good manager, you know how to access, process and absorb the information when you need it. There are two lessons we can learn from librarians here.

First, when new books arrive or existing books are returned to the library, the librarians don't immediately stop what they are doing and process the inbound books. Rather, under normal circumstances, they will accumulate books for a few hours (or days) before stopping to process them and put them on the shelves. We should do the same thing with much of our inbound datastream.

In the early days of e-mail, each inbound message on AOL was announced with a sing-songy little voice proclaiming, "You've got mail." I know a guy who used to instantly react to each and every such announcement. People who check and/or react to their in-basket on a real time basis today will never get anything else done. Think about it. If your mailman stopped at your desk every five minutes all day long, every day to drop off a single piece of correspondence, would you immediately stop what you were doing and deal with it? Of course not! So don't become a slave to your in-basket. Make it serve you, not the other way around.

Second, use a system for sorting and processing incoming matter. I try to deal with incoming information (e-mails, reports, snail mail, etc.) three times per day. I'll make the first pass on it about an hour after my arrival at work. I try not to do it first thing because I've got a list of things I'm trying to get done and want to achieve some positive momentum for the day before anything has a chance to get me off stride. The second pass is usually from my iPhone sometime during the lunch hour, and the last one is right before I go home at day's end.

As I go through the pile, as mentioned earlier, I'm looking first for things that are "mission critical." I will at least read those items and try to deal with them right then. "Dealing with them" might mean asking for more information, asking someone else to research or follow up on an item, sending a quick reply or taking other action. If it's something that is more complex and will require a re-read or more than a few minutes of additional thought, I'll take it home with me. I've made it a rule, though, no more than two hours of homework per night, three on a weekend. Since the world will always want more of your time than you have, you will need to set and keep rules that work for you. You will drown if you rely on others to do it for you.

Sort everything, and I mean everything else into files, or what I call "bins." I've got bins for the following items: Client Projects, Deals in Progress, Don't Do, Friends & Family, Interesting Stuff, Investments, Processed Mail, Read at Leisure, Receipts & Records, Recreation,

Travel, and To-Do's. If an item is categorized as a "To-Do," I list it as an appointment with a fixed time and date on my calendar. This is also the place where I keep follow-up copies of items I've tasked others with attending to or things that have been dumped … um … *delegated* to me. You probably noticed that I included a "Don't Do" bin. This is where I deposit things I'm choosing to ignore and thus have no intention of acting upon. The operative principle here is that some fires will just have to burn themselves out.

My bin categories include personal items. Here's the deal. My sense is that we've now reached the point where the line between one's business and personal life is sufficiently blurred that if it's okay for me to be regularly attending to work in my "off hours," and I do, then it is permissible (and rational) to attend to some personal matters during the business day. Hence, in my three daily visits to the mailbag, I deal with things from both categories. So there!

Sort the pepper from the flysh★t. Just as picnickers must learn to distinguish what's desirable from what's not, you must decide and let others know what information matters to you. Let people you work with know what your IP (information preferences) are. If you prefer short, bulleted reports and responses, set the example, and where possible, ask others to follow. When they do, let them know you really appreciate it. If they don't get it right away, or fall off the wagon, show them again.

> *Let people you work with know what your information preferences are.*

Train them to understand your mail-handling protocol so they won't expect instantaneous responses. In a similar vein, I know this is heresy to many of you, but I try hard to avoid texting business correspondence simply because it's understood to be a more fluid (real-time) medium. I just don't want to set myself or someone else up to be routinely firing stuff back and forth with the expectation that I will be responding instantly. Doing so suggests that neither of us has anything more important to do at the moment, which is almost universally untrue.

While we're on the topic, or close to it, the notion that each of us can simultaneously handle multiple tasks (multitask) is more fantasy than reality. That is certainly the case with anything that involves listening, to wit many organizations are banning the extraneous use of PDA's and laptops for communications during meetings. Taking notes on your device of choice or using it as a resource when a question comes up is one thing. Attending to your e-mail or surfing the net in the midst of a meeting keeps you from being fully present. Moreover, it is rude.

Do	Don't
Streamline your own output.	Spam people (this includes broadcast cc's).
Keep it positive, professional. Pick bones in person.	Flame people or engage in e-mail wars.
Seek limited input.	Get on lists that aren't absolutely relevant.
Seek to understand (challenge if need be) recurring data requests.	Set up recurring reports without a compelling, well-understood reason.

We think that once you're proficient at staying on top of your data stream, you'll find more (and better) opportunities to think. Good thinking requires focus and a *commitment* to *make* time to think. Acknowledge it. Accept it. Deal with it.

What to Think About?

The next time you successfully create for yourself some thinking time, here are some things to consider:

+ How you'll help a promising team member develop further.

+ What the members of your team need right now, and what they're going to need over the next year or so to do their very best work.

+ The solutions to some of your most "fixable"challenges and who will have good ideas about the tougher ones.

+ What you could start doing now (that you've never done before), that would make a positive difference in your work and those around you.

+ How you could take a measure of complexity out of some of your processes without sacrificing (and probably enhancing) results.

+ Who on your team doesn't get enough recognition and how you could correct that.

Thinking Is Legitimate Work

Good leaders have proven to themselves that thinking is legitimate work. It adds real value; failure to think costs real money. Understanding this helps us do our best thinking, but of even greater importance, it allows us, as leaders, to create an environment, a culture, where thinking is encouraged. Better yet, where thinking is required.

Thinking – good, clear, productive, breakthrough kind of thinking – is *hard work*. Well, it is for us, anyway. It's exhausting in a good way. We're not talking about daydreaming. But flat-out considering, weighing, pondering, designing, brainstorming, deciphering, reflecting, concluding, visualizing, and learning. All that is hard work. Don't let anyone tell you otherwise.

But because the task of thinking has, over the course of human history, garnered only minor respect relative to other kinds of work (heaving, toting, fashioning, scrubbing, drilling, typing, building, teaching, assembling, et. al.), many still don't *fully* classify thinking as true labor.

If you're one of those, think again.

Make the Time. Find the Place.

As mentioned earlier, the constant flood of messages to which we're subjected daily provides a never-ending opportunity to receive input. But until and unless we make time to do the processing, our minds resemble a sink with the faucet running and a clogged drain.

For all its accessibility, one place that may be the least conducive to productive thinking is … your cubicle or office. It's a natural breeding ground for distractions, teeming with phone calls, e-mails, texts, tweets, twirps, and all manner of demands, legitimate or not, for your attention. Even if you work at home in an otherwise empty house, the diversions are legion.

Get a Room!

As is the case with a few other things, thinking is best done in private. Of course, you gather the necessary input – "thinking fodder" we call it – from others. Talk things out and listen, listen, listen. But the actual thinking is a solo act. Because of that, there's simply no substitute for a venue that's quiet, comfortable and free from distractions.

Here are a few suggestions, based on what's worked for us:

+ **Airplanes.** Resist the urge to plug in, log on or make friends. Take earplugs and a book – paper or electronic (even if it's only a prop). Don't engage your seatmates in conversation. You don't have to be rude about it. Just stake your claim to some quiet time.

✦ **Your favorite coffee shop.**

✦ **A public library.** I'm writing this chapter from one right now.

✦ **Other public (kind of) places,** such as large hotel lobbies, places of worship (meditation is thinking), convention centers (the vast empty parts that are open but aren't being used much these days), gardens, and museums. If you're careful not to run afoul of security and don't abuse what may admittedly be squatter's status, you'll usually find nobody minds (or even notices) your being there. Thinking rarely disturbs those around us.

✦ **The great outdoors.** Surely there's a park or other quiet spot near you, some place you can go without being arrested for trespassing, and where others can't trespass on your need — your *right* — to do some good, clear thinking.

"Go Dark" to Develop Thinking on Your Team

While going dark, unplugging and untethering all have great benefits for our own thinking, these practices have much wider reach in making it easier — or at least possible — for others to practice the habit of thinking.

Just because we *can* be constantly available to our team members doesn't mean we *should* be. It's good for them and for us when we periodically (usually with advance notice) make ourselves unavailable for a few hours or days. Indeed, one of the things that has compromised professional development over the last decade is the fact that our bosses are seemingly always in the loop.

> *Just because we **can** be constantly available to our team members doesn't mean we **should** be.*

There's no benefit to hiding your intention here. Tell people, in clear terms, that you'll be offline for the next however long, and that you have every confidence that they'll make good choices during the time that you, in essence, don't exist to them. Obviously you'll want to have prepared them, over time, to handle what might come up. So-called "empowerment" minus preparation equals abandonment. But if you've prepared the ground, planted the seeds, and nourished your team's growth, you should be able to walk away and let them think.

Start by telling them you *want* them to think. Then reward them when they do. Strongly resist the temptation to punish them when they *do* think and it doesn't turn out well.

When interviewing someone for a job, assess their thinking skills and let them know before they get on the team that thinking is part – a big part – of the job they'll be doing. And just as we hope you've convinced yourself that it's okay (in fact, required) for you to take thinking time, let them know that you expect them to take thinking time, too. And that because you honor the time they'll spend thinking, you expect to see some results of that effort.

Give people "thinking assignments." We're serious. Do this individually or with a group. Sit down with someone on your team and tell her you'd like her to think about a very specific problem that has been the topic of discussion at several recent team meetings. Ask her to think about the problem and the following specific considerations:

1. The implications of the problem

2. Its possible causes

3. Its effects

4. A handful of plausible (that is, doable) responses that might solve the problem

Give her the gift of thinking time. Suggest some of the venues we recommended above. Give her three days to complete the assignment (she probably won't begin until day three and won't need more than one day, but you've given her three). Ask her to document her thinking on all four of the above elements and come back prepared to discuss with you her thinking. Be careful, though. The assignment is *not* to solve the problem. You'll need to emphasize this when making the assignment. Her task here is to *think it through*.

Why go through all of this? For one simple reason: accountability.

How often have we promised, "I'll give that some thought," and then give it not so much as a moment's consideration? Thinking, as we've said, is real work. It's a definable activity that produces results. It's reasonable and productive to ask people to spend time thinking, to record those thoughts, and share them with you.

Monday Morning 8 a.m.

1. Identify four accessible places outside your regular work venue that would be conducive to your thinking more effectively. Schedule a visit to one of them this week.

2. List three important issues that would benefit from your spending good thinking time. Make the time. Record your thoughts on paper, computer or voice recorder in a way that you can easily access and use later. Make this a habit.

3. Give a thinking assignment such as the one outlined above.

CHAPTER

7

FRIENDING:
BUILDING AND SUSTAINING VITAL NETWORKS

In the folk story *Stone Soup*, a shortage of food and other basic provisions had driven the residents of a village to hoard every morsel of food. One day, two soldiers arrived in the village and asked about staying in town for the night. They were advised to move on, as there wasn't a bite to eat in the village.

The soldiers said, "Oh, don't worry about that. In fact, we were going to make some stone soup and share it with all of you."

As the villagers puzzled about this thing called "stone soup," the soldiers filled a large cauldron with water, placed it over a fire, and then introduced an ordinary stone to the simmering pot.

As interest in the strange concoction began to brew throughout the village, one soldier allowed that while stone soup was itself quite tasty, it was hard to beat stone soup with a little cabbage in it. One villager managed to find a head of cabbage at home and contributed it to the cause. The other soldier recalled a particularly delicious batch of stone soup that had been flavored with meat, which jogged the memory of another villager, who went home and rustled up some salt beef he had squirreled away.

The smell of the soup led other villagers to think how nice it would be with just a few onions, mushrooms, and carrots, all of which, when they looked especially hard, they were able to find in their cupboards.

After the mayor remembered some potatoes he'd been saving for the right occasion, and added them to the pot, the soldiers produced a hearty meal for the whole village. So thankful were the villagers that they offered to pay the soldiers for the magic stone. But they would accept nothing for the recipe, and instead moved on to the next town at sunrise.

This story, in all its cultural variations, teaches us with simple elegance that we have, collectively, all we need to make our way. It's perhaps the earliest recorded story of networking – bringing our varied resources together for the benefit of all.

Stone Soup and Social Media

Everyone is building social networks these days – the bigger, the better, some say. In the new workspace, building relationships, inside and outside your organization, is critical to your success. How can you find new team players, mentors, advocates, resources and innovative ideas? How do you best encourage others to engage with you?

Some think the greater the number of "friends" you collect, the more your prestige, importance and ability to get things you want. But, collecting is only the first step in building a vital network. Until you offer something others care about (e.g. information, opportunities, creative ideas, humor, trust, support, candor), your outreach will prove annoying and unproductive, regardless of the setting.

Successful leadership works the same way. It isn't about *getting*. Great leadership is about giving such meaningful value to others that they want to invest with you and follow your guidance (vs. ignore, block, delete or diss you to everyone in their network).

Do an honest assessment of your friending practices, and look at how "me centered" your efforts are. If in more than 25 percent of the cases you are reaching out to others

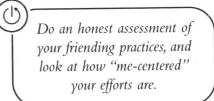

Do an honest assessment of your friending practices, and look at how "me-centered" your efforts are.

solely or largely because of what they can do for you, we suggest you start looking through the other end of the lens.

Leading is fundamentally about relating in ways that others perceive can help them achieve their goals. People want leaders who will open better futures. The leaders to whom they are most loyal are those who treat them with the respect of friends, who show interest in and appreciate them, offer assistance, tell them the truth – even when it is hard – listen (really listen) to them, support them in tough times, and value what they contribute. How do you stack up?

While leadership isn't primarily about making friends (and sometimes costs you friends), there are lessons from social media that can help you lead successfully in the new world.

Finding Friends

The better the people you work with, the better the results you can achieve and the more fun you can have. How do you "friend" them effectively? With social media, you begin with your known network and use them to grow new connections. When he was hired, John was challenged to turnaround results within six months. The first thing he did was build his network. His choice to start by getting to know others, understanding their roles, priorities and concerns, and offering to help them before he asked for their help, saved weeks of time and headaches over the months that followed. Here are a few of his tips for building your network:

Improves Network Building	Crashes the Network
Express interest in knowing and listening to others.	Expect that people will friend you before they know you.
When others accept your invitation, welcome them.	Ignore when others express interest in or sign on with you.
Learn what others care about and ask how you can help them succeed.	Give others whatever *you* think is cool and important. Bore, offend or irritate them.
When others contact you or ask for help, respond promptly and usefully. If you can't, let them know and suggest someone who can help.	Blow others off when they contact you. Think they will understand your delays or silences.

In short, in rebooted leadership, it's about *them*, about *us*, and what we can do together. It is not about *you*. Consistently search for great alliances, potential core and virtual team members and mentors before you need them. Pay it forward. Express interest in others and how they might benefit from association, and generously offer to help them succeed. You'll pique their interest and begin the journey to success for everyone.

Strengthening Friendships

How do you keep relationships vital, when the day-to-day grind wears everyone down? Remember the story of the wife who complained to her husband that he never told her that he loved her anymore? (In case you don't, he replied with amazement, "What do you mean? I told you I loved you when we married. I'll let you know if I ever change my mind.")

You, too, must invest consistently and meaningfully in sustaining the vitality of key relationships to keep them fresh and strong. Basic lessons from kindergarten provide great guidance. Play nice, share your things, tell people what you like about them, and don't do mean things.

Beyond these, use the same practices you use for managing projects. Know others' goals, maintain regular contact, check how things are working, explore how you can improve, make clear agreements and minimize surprises, celebrate successes, and clear up any breakdowns quickly. Bottom line, invest in keeping your network active, interesting, fun, and beneficial to all.

Improves Relationships	Crashes Relationships
Act generously.	Take others for granted.
Listen, appreciate and give what others value, generously.	Give what you want or think others want vs. what they truly value.
Keep a schedule of regular contact. (Make the time.)	Let connections happen when there is time – they won't.
Celebrate progress, efforts and successes with others.	Overlook efforts, progress and successes.
When you've goofed, apologize and start again.	Pretend you're perfect.

Leading Your Former Peers

Sustaining relationships when you shift roles from colleague to boss or from boss of one project to member on another can get messy. When you become a leader, roles and rules change for all.

If being a leader were to be known by other words, those words would be "higher expectations." Higher expectations for conduct, judgment, courage, vision, and communication. As a leader, your performance is more visible. Your duty to listen increases exponentially. Sadly, no one can bestow the ability to succeed in one day, but the following ideas can help address three important friending challenges:

1. **When you change roles,** the rules regarding friends change, too. Your behavior is governed by a new standard. As a case in point, you can't date the help. Repeat, you cannot date the help. Nor can you be as open and casual as before. For one thing, you are no longer speaking just for yourself. Your comments and commitments will be taken as representative of and binding on the larger organization. Hence, it is vital to quickly understand and embrace the new dynamics, rules, expectations, and responsibilities.

2. **Non-negotiable roles.** As a leader, you must keep some information confidential and make some tough calls, alone. You will be expected to support ideas and convey messages from your bosses that you don't particularly agree with. You will assess performance, decide consequences, and deliver tough news to people you consider to be friends. Clarifying your roles and responsibilities up front will help you avoid confusion and conflict later. This does not mean that you give up your identity or values. Rather, that in accepting a leadership role, you are expected to think and act beyond the end of your own nose.

3. **Friending up.** (Note: This does not equate to sucking up.) Standard advice for entering any community (online or otherwise) is to "listen first." It's also good advice in getting to know your new boss(es). Some things to learn:

   ✦ Their goals and aspirations for themselves and their organization(s)

   ✦ Their expectations for you and your team

+ Their likes, dislikes and interests

+ Their preferences for connecting, for getting feedback, for disagreeing

+ Best ways to irritate them

Remember, your job is to listen, show interest and offer your support. Invite the connections, appreciate and build them through good times and bad. Use your network to stay current about senior leaders and their challenges so you can provide them with real value. Make sure that the only surprises you give them are good ones.

Fighting With Friends

Conflict will increase as your team is more mobile, more diverse, and faces bigger challenges with more limited resources. Moreover, the increased presence of social media makes it possible for conflict to get out of control faster than ever. Remember, with just 140 characters and a few RT's, a crowd (mob) can be gathered pretty quickly. Accordingly, it is to your advantage to become skillful at handling conflict productively and quickly. If you shy away from it, you'll miss opportunities for learning, creativity and strengthening relationships and results. If you engage in healthy "fighting," for the sake of making everyone better from the experience, you'll become a more effective leader.

Consider the difference between a street fighter and an Olympic boxer. Both fight, but for different reasons and with different rules. Fight like an Olympian: within confined boundaries, with appreciation for your opponent as someone committed to do well, and with whom you can both take your performance to a higher level. Compete to excel, and yes, to win, but not to crush or humiliate others.

Choose your battles wisely. Before you fight, ask yourself if the issue will still be important in six months. Fight about ethical and values violations and issues of strategic importance, but don't sweat the small stuff. Sometimes, hold your fire.

Karen was overwhelmed and forgot to deliver a report her boss expected to take to a client the next day. Her boss called her in and asked where it was. She confessed that she flat-out overlooked it, apologized deeply, and acknowledged that he had reason to fire her. No theatrics, no excuses, she just admitted a bad mistake and waited for the worst. Instead, he said, "If you're big enough to admit it, then I am big enough to leave it alone." His one act of holding fire earned Karen's loyalty for years.

Choose your battles wisely. Before you fight, ask yourself if the issue will still be important in six months.

Always fight in person and, whenever possible, in private. Yet, do not, repeat, do not make it personal. Fighting by e-mail — worse yet, fighting by e-mail and copying the world — is self-defeating and weakens your networks.

Here are some guidelines for fighting "fair:"

Builds Vitality and Creativity	Crashes Vitality and Creativity
Speak only about the current issue and resolve it.	Bring up ancient history to pile on evidence that breaks down the other person and the focus on the current issue.
Fight about the issues, facts, possibilities, risks and benefits. Fight to learn and improve.	Fight the person.
Honor differences in style and values across cultures, positions and generations.	Assume everyone is like and should be like you. Assume they are wrong and bad if they aren't.

Builds Vitality and Creativity	Crashes Vitality and Creativity
Ask questions: ✦ Why is their view important to them? ✦ What don't you understand yet? ✦ How are your views outdated or incomplete? ✦ Is there win–win potential?	Assume you know what the conflict is about. Convince the other person you are right. Insist it is your way or the highway.
Ask for what you want, clearly and simply. Stay future focused. Explain the benefits of your request.	Talk about what you don't want, what's not okay, what needs to stop. Focus on what's wrong vs. what can improve the situation.

Even though negative feedback may feel like the start of a fight, don't go there. Remember the companies that have made their reputations by making it easy to give them feedback: Nordstrom, L.L. Bean, Zappo's? It is one thing to make a mistake … they are inevitable. People will watch how well you recover from mistakes and respond to their feedback.

To strengthen relationships when others give you critical feedback, especially the unskillful kind, take a deep breath and pause. Choose to treat it as a well-intended gift. Even if you disagree with it, others' willingness to bring something of concern to your attention is valuable. Thank them. Summarize their feedback to assure you've understood their concerns. (Repeat until they confirm that you understand.)

If you agree with their feedback, thank them and say what you'll do to change. Ask them to tell you if you change appropriately. If you disagree, explain why you won't take their advice. Thank them again for bringing forward their ideas.

Learn to brush off some feedback. If it is ungrounded or an overreaction by someone highly emotional, let it go. This kind of feedback isn't about you. If it's heated, you can politely and firmly say, "Let's talk about this when things cool down so we can be more constructive." You can also let others know if they will need to adapt without you. This is important to do when others try to make you responsible for something instead of learning to address it themselves.

Finishing "Friendships" – TTYL
Staff transitions, bosses change, clients shift and you may move, too. How do you say "goodbye" and keep relationships strong?

The quick answer? Assume "goodbye" is temporary. Assume your paths will cross in the future, if not directly, then certainly indirectly. The impressions you leave at "goodbye" will follow your reputation and ability to engage others in the future. Choose well.

When Others Leave
Regardless of their timing, which can sometimes hurt badly, be polite. Thank them for their contributions and wish them well. Take the high road. When possible, help them leave. Open doors to new opportunities, give recommendations, and make introductions to people who can support their careers. They will always remember your assistance.

Regroup as fast as you can. Use your network, and ask for help. If you can't find a new person, ask the people you rely on to absorb greater responsibility. Try to avoid taking them on yourself. If others add responsibilities, work to ease their loads in other ways, as a friend would do. Help them prioritize effectively. If you can't ease their responsibilities, do all you can to appreciate them and see that they are appropriately recognized.

Speak favorably about people who've made good contributions. If you never mention them again, others will predict they will get the same treatment. Don't give them reasons to believe they are cogs in your machine rather than valued colleagues. Many companies are known for keeping "alumni" active as networking resources. Build your personal alumni group for similar value. You can never have too many good supporters.

When You Must Ask Others to Leave

You can't lead successfully unless you are willing to release people who don't contribute adequately. One of the most draining leadership mistakes is keeping people who are not carrying their weight. As soon as you let them go, you'll see everyone's spirits rise. It is never fun and sometimes heartbreaking, but it is your job to do it well.

> *You can't lead successfully unless you are willing to release people who don't contribute adequately.*

Do	Don't
If a person doesn't fit, make a change, sooner rather than later.	Get sucked into trying to build a case on nonexistent performance issues.
If performance issues are at stake, ensure the person has had fair and ample opportunity to succeed.	Overlook your own culpability for poor performance management.
Allow the person to "fall on their own sword" (resign with honor).	Make it even harder and messier than it has to be.

Do	Don't
Realize that as a manager you get paid to deal affirmatively with those who don't fit or measure up.	Let firing people become easy or routine. If it ceases to bother you, find something else to do.
Realize that how you treat people on their way out is being watched by a lot of others who are simultaneously forming an opinion about how you would treat them under similar circumstances.	Neglect to seek and strongly consider the advice of a competent HR professional.
Say as little as possible publicly.	Tweet and tell.

When You Leave

Leaving a position can be tricky. Consider what you want people to say about how you handled leaving. Were you loyal or did you throw trash as you left? Did you whine or did you stay appreciative? Be proud of your choices when word goes around about your transitioning style.

Assess your organization's culture to help you decide the best timing. If you work at a place that will ask you to leave as soon as you announce, that is one situation. If your organization will help make a smooth transition, that is another. Ask your mentor how to best handle your leave taking.

In short, make your transition as easy as you can on the people left behind. Speak with those who need to know and no one else until the transition is planned with your boss. Appreciate whatever you are grateful for as you leave, and after you're gone.

Summary

In the new world, you won't have all the resources you want under your personal control. The only way to optimize your resources is by creating, strengthening and transitioning relationships really well. What help do you need? Who can provide it? How can you find them and build a mutually supportive connection? Reach out and begin friending soon and consistently.

Monday Morning 8 a.m.

1. Write down the names of 10 people who are most important to your success in the coming year. Set a plan and schedule for building your relationships with them.

2. Notice your impact on people today. Do they approach you, avoid you, comply without engagement, hide things, show enthusiasm? Now take 100 percent responsibility for their mood and behavior. What do you contribute to them? What one thing would you consider a "best practice" that encourages a strong, creative and inspiring connection? What one thing might you change to engage people more powerfully? Do it today.

CHAPTER

8

FAILING

The lost customer. The breakdown that broke your budget. The promotion denied. The big presentation that bombed. The critical resources refused. The teammate who went rogue. What are *your* toughest failures?

Stuff Happens

Being a leader requires facing failure as an unavoidable reality. It will happen and it will hurt. And it will happen again. Your success (and that of your followers) hinges upon picking your way through the wreckage and getting back on course quickly, and with a modicum of grace. So ...

- ✦ What risks should you choose to take?

- ✦ How do you fail without letting it sink you?

- ✦ How do you handle your failures so that you gain, rather than lose precious credibility and respect?

Your boss holds high expectations for your performance. Your team's mistakes threaten her success. If you fail, she gets the heat. You may get something worse.

As a manager, you face a dilemma. Your job is to stay predictable and stable, to incrementally improve things without risking big mistakes. Yet, to succeed, you must sometimes risk beyond what is known and predictable. Sometimes, you will come up short.

Success in the new world requires you to:

- Extend trust to others, include others' ideas, encourage their creativity, and rely on them to deliver. Sometimes, they will fail you.

- Rely on people you don't know personally. You must risk that their style, competence and integrity will advance your goals. Sometimes they won't.

- Innovate and deliver unproven ideas that may or may not yield profit. When successful, you may or may not get the credit.

- Work long hours to achieve goals that may change before you achieve success.

How do you navigate between the "rock" of driving for success and the "hard place" of knowing that you will occasionally fail? Carefully.

When to Risk Failing
How do you choose when, what kind, and how big a risk to take? Consider these guidelines:

Decide how badly you need this job. If you are the sole breadwinner with three kids, have no financial cushion, or see retirement looming and are uncertain of your ability to quickly find a new gig, playing it "safe" may be your best option. In many roles, risking conservatively is fine. Be sure you are in one.

Assess how much risk your boss and your organization will tolerate. What is the culture of your organization and the style of your boss? If they are hard driving with high standards and demand strong egos that love swimming with sharks, decide if that is for you. The rewards and the costs can be high. If you like this, button your chin strap, risk wisely, work your tail off, learn as fast as you can, and enjoy the adventure. If your boss and organization are conservative, you may want to be cautious. If you don't like what you observe, keep your network active. You may want to choose a different situation.

Check your boss's and company's style for developing leaders. How do they support leaders who take stretch assignments? Do they allow learning by failing? If they do, push yourself to step up to new challenges, and know when to hit the "help button" to avoid catastrophic failure. Take risks that will let you learn quickly, as long as they won't suck all the oxygen out of the room if something goes wrong. If you risk wisely, do your best, avoid surprising key players, support your team, and learn from every experience, you should be fine. If your context doesn't encourage learning through risking, decide how much you want this job.

Know if someone will unfairly claim credit for successes and blame you for mistakes. If the culprit is a peer or teammate on whom you must rely, find a way to mitigate the risk. If it's your boss, seriously consider finding a new situation. Work for sponsors who will open doors, support your ideas, and cover your back. Without these people, your career advancement will likely be slower and more limited.

Stay crystal clear about your personal values, aspirations, commitments. What really is most important to you? If it is "getting" more, e.g., money, visibility, promotions, recognition, then you may be disappointed in the new world. Yes, you must have a healthy drive for success, and we aren't suggesting that you emulate Mother Teresa, but you will get farther (and more) by playing nicely with others and putting their interests at least on par with your own. Risks for purely personal gain will jeopardize you. Risks for creating value with and for others can help everyone.

Choose Wise Risks	Choose Bad Risks
Take risks you'd be proud to read about on the Internet.	Do something illegal, immoral or unethical. (You will get caught.)
Tell people who might be negatively impacted what you are doing and gain their upfront support.	Experiment with something big that your boss hasn't approved.
Keep key people up to date on your progress and any setbacks. Avoid surprising them.	Blindside your important stakeholders.

Be Your Best When Failure Hits

Failing arrives with a specific event. It hurts in your gut and changes your world. Period.

More than once, as a young manager, I let stress and frustration turn me into a tyrant. I developed a habit of "managing by outburst," berating team members for all that wasn't going according to plan. Immediately after one particularly harsh (and apparently loud) declamation, my boss, Greg, (the best leader I ever had) called me into his office and fed me a dose of much-needed humility.

He made it clear that my behavior was causing me to lose the respect of my team, and that my tirades and general bad temper were sucking out productivity at a time we could ill afford it. He didn't say much else. He didn't have to.

I went home that night and thought. Greg's use of the "R" word – respect, had captured my attention. The next day, I went to each team member and apologized. I didn't grovel, but I think most knew I meant it. I worked hard at change. It was neither easy nor perfect, but it happened.

From this experience, I learned:

- ✦ My behavior wasn't okay, and relapsing wouldn't be, either.
- ✦ To find a release valve before exploding on those I care about.
- ✦ People forgive when they see real contrition.
- ✦ Not to hold others to a higher standard than I do myself.
- ✦ If you call someone your best leader ever, listen to them.

But, failing is relative, too. How it impacts you depends on your self-confidence, your view of your situation, and your attitudes about life. Here are some valuable lessons from successful leaders on building resilience:

Get back on your feet and be your best, quickly. Life guarantees us pain. No one escapes. It is truly a pay-me-now or pay-me-later phenomenon. Like exercising too soon after an injury, un–healed emotional pain can lead to continuing breakdowns. Emotional pain appears as irritability, depression and exhaustion, and can linger for years if you don't invest in healing. Exhale, experience pain, and give yourself what helps you recover. Hint: Things like focusing intently on a goal and being kind to others help immensely.

In contrast to pain, suffering is optional. Witness Vietnam-era U.S. Naval aviator Charlie Plumb, who flew 74 successful combat missions over north Vietnam and made over 100 carrier landings. On his 75th mission, just five days before the end of his tour, Plumb was shot down over Hanoi, taken prisoner, tortured, and spent the next 2,103 days as a POW. Today, Capt. Plumb speaks to leadership audiences about how he initially suffered and then chose to move past a "woe is me" attitude brought on by being shot down in a war that he didn't start.

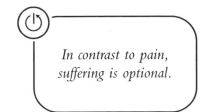

In contrast to pain, suffering is optional.

Suffering happens when we extend the memory of pain with our thinking. While asking questions of "what if," "why me," and "what could have been different" may be important for learning, we disable ourselves if we recycle them endlessly and relive the failures. Find your way past these restraining thoughts as soon as possible. Here are some ways that can help:

Use your e-motions. Emotions are "e-motions" or energy for motion. Feel them and then use their energy to start recovering. Consider the questions: How would I advise my best friend in this situation? How would a great leader advise me? What could I become without self-defeating thoughts? Reconnect with what is most important to you. Motivate yourself with your long-term vision and goals. Write out your personal and team resources, then use what you learn to start making constructive choices.

"Shrink the game." Baseball players generate peak performance over a long season by focusing on one pitch, one at-bat, or one play at a time. They zero in on what is most important right now. Shift your focus away from the disappointments, and shrink your game to that next step for rebuilding successfully. Make your next decisions and actions winning moments and you will build a winning game.

Sometimes your best is getting out of bed every morning. Other times, you can reconnect and act on your passion for contributing usefully and boldly. We can be guided by the examples of amazing people like Nancy G. Brinker, who founded Susan G. Komen for the Cure, in memory of her sister, and Candice Lightner, founder of MADD, who used their pain as a generator for starting powerful social movements. Pull together all the help you can find. Nourish your spirit generously and move forward with courage. Do

> *Sometimes your best is getting out of bed every morning. Other times, you can reconnect and act on your passion for contributing usefully and boldly.*

what builds your pride and you will increase the odds of success exponentially.

Rebound Powerfully	Maximize the Suffering
Reconnect with what is most important and who can help.	Prolong your funk.
Make amends. Repair what you can.	Ignore the messes you've made.
Invite feedback, and learn to improve.	Replay your disappointment, anger or sadness on a continuous loop so it pervades your mood, everywhere and all the time.
Move through remorse, shame, or anger. Release what you can't control, then move on.	Assume that the pain and impact of failing are permanent. Discount your opportunities to change.

Failing Can Benefit You

Strengthen your resilience muscles. Ted was at risk of losing a key client. It was hard to imagine the consequence of this potential loss to him, his team and the future of his organization. When asked how he was coping, he replied, "My wife died of cancer much too young. I lost my first business venture after my partner made a fatal mistake. Two huge blows and I am still here.

"At those times, life seemed over. I had no blooming idea what good could come next. In both cases, my future became better than I ever could have imagined. As a result, I've learned to relax when hard times hit. I keep opening doors, stay passionate about what I value, and hang around good people. I've learned I can't know the future, but I am now sure it is going to surprise me with better than I can imagine." Ted has mastered "resilience."

Leaders are those who are at their best when others are often at their worst. While others are frantic, they are calm in the storm. They project clarity and resourcefulness in the midst of impossible situations. That capability only comes from practice.

The more times you recover, the more easily you'll find good ways to handle challenges you face and the more confident you'll be that you can handle whatever comes your way. Embrace stretch experiences that help you learn to handle the unknowns you'll face.

Build compassion. You hear those who have suffered big losses, pain, health issues or failures say, "You don't know until you've been there." Once you've met personal failures, you more easily relate to others in similar situations. You'll know when to provide practical help. You'll feel comfortable just being "present" when nothing else helps. You'll know when to use humor and when to use tough love, and how to apply them with an appreciation of the difficulties others face.

Many of the most-respected and successful leaders have lived through considerable adversity and emerged stronger. Adversity "done well" is a source of wisdom, courage and comfort in your own skin that is hard to attain otherwise. When you hate failing but handle it well, recovering effectively when it hits, you have a leadership resource that is invaluable. Others will want to work with and for you to create their futures.

Monday Morning 8 a.m.

1. Check the kinds of risks you are taking. Given your personal needs, your environment and the future you want to help build, decide if you are taking enough of the right kind. Name one way you can risk more wisely and follow through.

2. Check your attitude. Are you carrying around old anger, remorse or a sense of defeat that limits your enthusiasm, contribution and impact? Decide what you can do to release any you find, then move on without them.

3. Notice who fails constructively and who doesn't on your team. Think of one way you can help those who shrink from failing to build their courage and resilience. Consider inviting a senior leader to come in and speak about failures that helped shape their success.

9

INFLUENCING IN A SOUND-BITE WORLD

To achieve your goals in the new workspace, you must engage clients, staff, bosses, and team members with competing priorities. Influencing is more important and harder now. Why?

- ✦ Flatter organizations require you to interact with a broader group of leaders. With fewer middle managers:

  - ✧ Senior leaders may ask directly for your status and ideas. If they ask you to attend a senior team meeting, how prepared are you?

  - ✧ You more often will go directly to a senior leader for help. No more sending issues "up the ladder" and letting your boss handle them.

- ✦ Leaders from other departments who depend on your team expect you to fix problems. No buffers from "above."

- ✦ Changes hit your team faster, often as surprises. Your staff faces re-structuring, new bosses, changing priorities and budgets, new delivery standards and perhaps, "we've been bought by a competitor."

✦ You lead a broader range of generations, cultures and backgrounds. Generation Y may want your direction and feedback on their schedules, often "now." Boomers may want to work autonomously and challenge your decisions and feedback. Are you ready to influence these diverse audiences?

✦ You are increasingly responsible for advancing your own career. Your bosses and mentors may not have the time or ability to help. How can you shape your own career and influence staff, peers, leaders and clients to support you?

If you are struggling to influence in the "big leagues," read on.

Influencing Senior Leaders

When top leaders invite you to a senior team meeting, do your research, prepare a clear, compelling presentation and operate like a member of their "tribe." Anticipate their reactions and how you'll respond so you'll know when to course-correct and when you've won or lost.

As a young manager, a senior team member invited me to introduce the results of a focus group recommending controversial changes. I readied a compelling multimedia show, and after just two minutes of it, the CEO slammed the table, turned off the presentation, and barked his displeasure that the issues presented were happening in the company. He insisted that everyone at the table take specific actions to fix them and report back at the following meeting. Somehow, I completely missed what had happened and stood up to continue my well-rehearsed presentation. I didn't realize I'd won until, mercifully, a friendly leader signaled me to stop and sit down.

If you want to influence senior leaders more effectively, here are some great reminders.

Influence Like a Pro	Crash and Burn
Do your homework — rigorously. Know your topic and the top concerns of your audience.	Wing it.
Present your information clearly, simply and concisely. Tell: ✦ Why the topic is important to *them*. ✦ What is most critical to know. ✦ Next steps and why they matter. If you can't explain it with a crayon, you'll fail.	Assume they know what they need to make a good decision. ✦ Skip setting clear context. ✦ Tell them what *you* think is important vs. what *they* value. ✦ Make your presentation complex and hard to follow.
Show up at your best. ✦ Use an engaging verbal or visual style. ✦ Show your enthusiasm. ✦ Respond to their concerns, ideas, suggestions, and demands. ✦ Sustain your composure under all circumstances.	Treat them like executioners vs. supporters. ✦ Worry about what they will think of you vs. what value you can give them. ✦ React emotionally. (They'll remember an emotional breakdown longer than any disagreements about content.)
Know when to fold 'em. ✦ Choose when to lose the battle so you might win the war. ✦ If you've gotten the green light, shut up and get off the stage.	Be inflexible and unwilling to be influenced. ✦ Resist others' views. ✦ Fight to the death — probably yours.

Influencing Diverse Audiences

You will increasingly face diversity of age, gender, culture, position, nationality, expertise and experience. You will need to engage everyone to achieve your goals and build loyal networks successfully. It can take the wisdom and patience of the Dalai Lama, but it is increasingly essential, and possible.

Next are some better practices for influencing diverse audiences:

Highly Influential	Shoot Yourself in the Foot
Be curious. Ask with sincere interest about others' experiences and orientations. ✦ What's your understanding of X? ✦ What is most important to you about X?	Assume you know what is right and best. ✦ State your positions before you understand others'. ✦ Criticize others publicly.
Stay curious and inclusive.	Assume you only need to ask once and others will tell you everything that is important to them about an entire situation.
Be adaptable: ✦ Work for win-win solutions. ✦ Enjoy stretching.	Insist that others adapt to you: ✦ Criticize them if they don't "get it" quickly. ✦ Speak louder, sarcastically or impatiently.
Stretch your media skills to communicate powerfully with all groups in their styles, not yours.	Ignore media, language and styles beyond what you know.
Assume positive intent – that others, certainly to include those who are different from you, have your best interest at heart.	Assume others intend to frustrate, challenge and limit your success.

Not everyone is like you or aspires to be like you. If you treat everyone as if they are, you'll limit your effectiveness severely. By mastering these skills, you'll earn respect for recognizing, valuing and making the most of similarities and differences. You'll expand your base of influence and bring big dividends to your results and career.

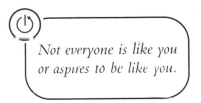

Not everyone is like you or aspires to be like you.

Earning "Table Pounder" Advocates

Ideally, you have strong sponsors who help advance your career. But given how stretched leaders are, this is less likely with each passing day. It is your job to assertively find and prepare your sponsors to support you.

Meetings to decide assignments and bonuses are often heated. You need skillful "table pounder" advocates who promote you if you hope to be chosen for opportunities.

How do you make it easy for others to advocate for you?

- ✦ Demonstrate consistently outstanding performance in all areas that matter most to your business and its leaders.

- ✦ Show you can succeed at the next level before you officially earn it.

- ✦ Build relationships with decision makers (see Chapter 7 – Friending) who strengthened their confidence and trust in your values, style and abilities.

- ✦ Look the part.

- ✦ Ensure they have no reasons to say "no."

Finally, learn to promote your and your team's strengths, capabilities and capacity using these four steps:

1. Identify two recent successes that demonstrate strong talents, resourcefulness, creativity and contributions. Practice how to

describe them in less than one minute using what follows. Write down your basic script.

2. When a leader asks how you are, respond with emotion (typically enthusiasm or relief) and tell only the bottom line impact you or your team delivered. This sounds like:

✦ "Great! Our team just learned we improved our quality metrics by X percent."

✦ "Tired and happy. We just fought hard and won an $X project."

Stop talking. You've made your case. If they ask, "How did you do that?" continue to the next step.

3. State the gap you closed (in 10 seconds), e.g.

✦ "We prioritized and eliminated our top two sources of quality breakdowns."

✦ "We heard about X client's issues and gave them a really compelling pitch for how we can solve them."

Stop talking. Laying out the before and after "gap" your team closed gives a compelling story to tell, "They know how to identify and address these kinds of challenges."

4. If a leader asks the third question, "How did you do that?" name the three competencies you want them to remember. Don't tell the long, detailed story of what happened. Present just these three highlights. Call out what you want them to remember and equip them to tell their peers clearly. Remember that describing your team's competence and success says as much about you as it does about them. Even better, you are seen as generous and a team leader.

✦ "We engaged everyone's ideas, got great advice from a Six Sigma Black Belt and stuck to hitting our goals no matter what."

◆ "We invested the upfront time to ensure our client believed we understood and cared about their needs. We set and implemented a detailed project plan to deliver on time, and then polished our presentation so it would blow their socks off."

Prepare and use this style of influencing on any accomplishment that can equip others to advocate for you. Merely hoping that leaders notice your successes won't work. Boasting "I did this and accomplished that" won't engage anyone, either. This approach is like fly fishing — lay an inviting lure in the water and if it is well placed, well timed and inviting, you'll eventually get a bite.

For even more detail, our favorite book on this topic is *Brag! How to Toot Your Own Horn Without Blowing It*, by Peggy Klaus.

As the world becomes increasingly complex and moves faster, it is even more important that you learn to listen, understand and respond to others effectively. Bottom line, your skillfulness as an *influencer* is a critical leadership competency that shapes your own, your team's, and your organization's success.

> Bottom line, your skillfulness as an **influencer** is a critical leadership competency that shapes your own, your team's, and your organization's success.

Learning to tell your story in a clear and authentic way that others can relate to, will do more for your career than another 50 I.Q. points, or 10 years of experience.

Monday Morning 8 a.m.

1. Review tips for interacting with senior leaders, assess yourself and choose one thing to improve this week. Practice it so you can improve before "showtime."

2. Name someone you want to influence. List three things that are most important to them about the change you want them to support. Bullet-point three convincing examples for how your proposed change will provide what they most want so you can "sell" them based on what they care about.

3. Ask someone you trust to name one way you might shut down others' ideas, contributions or enthusiasm and one thing you could do to improve. Thank them and start changing just that one thing.

4. Identify a success that would equip others to advocate for you. Write down your brag in the format above.

CHAPTER
10

PRESSING THE BUTTON

So there you have it. Your job as a leader has not been made any easier by the social, economic and political upheaval of the past decade. But, as something of a bright side, you can take heart in knowing that your role has not been declared redundant or irrelevant. Far from it. What you do is more vital now than it has been for a long time.

We've discovered yet again that short cuts, shenanigans and spin don't work very long, if at all. Moreover, they come at a price similar to what occurs when a computer is burdened with all kinds of extraneous junk. You wake up one day and notice that it is running more slowly and less reliably, and crashing more. You clean it up, reboot, and go on.

That's where we are as leaders of businesses and other organizations. We're in the process of rebooting. Our organizations cannot do it. It is up to each of us as individuals.

Whether by listening more (a lot more) or discharging those who have had one too many ethical lapses, it is up to us to restore trust.

We must take the difficult and often lonely step of bringing more truth to the table, whether doing performance reviews, or reminding senior leaders that a pig wearing lipstick is still a pig.

We must be ever more skillful at building our own networks, staffed with talented folks who recognize real value in getting sticky with us.

We must make (and take) time to think, affording our teammates the very same latitude, and in the process, stretch and strengthen our critical thinking skills.

Realizing that we are more responsible than ever for our own development, we must take steps to build both skills and resilience. We should make it a point to practice in bad weather and associate with those who will challenge and care enough to tell us the truth.

We must learn to rebound from the failures that inevitably happen, and to modestly but effectively shine a light on our accomplishments.

We sincerely hope that we have made your path in the new world just a little brighter.

Get going.

ACKNOWLEDGEMENTS

As authors, we often wonder if anyone reads the acknowledgements page of a book, apart from those being acknowledged, their families and friends. In this case, we hope you *are* reading this page, because we are extremely grateful to those without whom this book would not have progressed beyond the thinking stage we refer to in Chapter 6 (You Get Paid to Think!).

Thank you, Steve Browne of LaRosa's Pizza, and founder of the HR Net; Tim Kern of Pfizer; Steve Lishansky of Optimize International; Rob Morris of Alaska Children's Services; Dawn Peters of Naked Health Group; Nancy Robinson of Mrs. Robinson Cooks; Sue Seboda of Congressional Motors; and James Wright of Pulsar Advertising. Your comments and guidance helped shape what became *Rebooting Leadership*.

Thank you to the readers of our blogs and online newsletters, who help keep us on track with what's most important in the world of people strategy. And a special thanks to our readers and subscribers who completed a survey we conducted early in the process of writing this book. You guided and focused our thinking as to which of the many possible leadership topics to pursue.

And thanks to our own team, Karen Calabrese, Kristi Shea and Betty Cottle Hadden, who work with us in our respective offices, doing the things they're good at (and that we're not), and who keep us showing up prepared and looking smarter than we really are.

And, finally, thanks to our families and friends, those who support us, encourage us and prod us, and who seem to know exactly when we need each of the aforementioned actions.

ABOUT THE AUTHORS

Meredith Kimbell is founder and president of Corporate Adventure, headquartered in Reston, Va. She consults nationally with start-ups, mid-tier, and Fortune 500 companies to improve performance, profits and fulfillment. She assists leaders and teams to define and consistently deliver their most important results. She improves communications, accelerates successful change, and facilitates mission-critical meetings. She is a consultant, advisor, coach, facilitator, and source of inspiration to her clients.

(703) 471-7745   corporateadventure.com   meredith@rebootingleadership.com

Richard Hadden, is co-author, with Bill Catlette, of *Contented Cows Give Better Milk* and *Contented Cows Moove Faster*. He has managed teams in financial services and information technology. Since 1989, he has consulted with, trained, and spoken for hundreds of organizations on five continents. He has a management degree from Jacksonville University and an MBA from the University of North Florida. He lives in his native Jacksonville, Fla.

(904) 720-0870   contentedcows.com   richard@rebootingleadership.com

Bill Catlette has more than 30 years' leadership experience in the corporate world and in his cutting-edge management consultancy. His corporate ports of call have included assignments with Genuine Parts Co. (NAPA), ADP and FedEx. A thought leader in the field of Human Workplace Performance, he is a frequent seminar leader, keynote speaker at business meetings, and executive coach. Bill lives near Memphis, Tenn.

(901) 853-9646   contentedcows.com   bill@rebootingleadership.com

3 Effective Ways to Help Reboot Leadership within Your Organization

1. Keynote Presentation
Invite the authors to keynote your next meeting and inspire your team to create greater success.
Contact www.**RebootingLeadership**.com

2. Workshop
Facilitated by a *Rebooting Leadership* author, during this 3- or 6-hour workshop participants will develop a personal action plan that can make an immediate and profound difference in their careers and lives.
Contact www.**RebootingLeadership**.com

3. PowerPoint™ Presentation
Enhance the *Rebooting Leadership* experience in your organization with this professionally produced PowerPoint™ Slide Deck and easy-to-follow Facilitator's Guide. Use the presentation to kick off meetings and training sessions, or as a follow-up reinforcement tool. **$99.95**
Downloadable from www.**CornerStoneLeadership**.com

Visit www.**CornerStoneLeadership**.com for additional books and resources.

Accelerate Powerful Leadership Package
$199.95

Order Form

1-30 copies $15.95   31-99 copies $14.95   100+ copies $13.95

Rebooting Leadership   ____ copies X _____   = $ _____

Rebooting Leadership PowerPoint™ Presentation ____ copies X $00.00   = $ _____

Additional Leadership Development Resources

Accelerate Powerful Leadership Package   ____ pack(s) X $199.95   = $ _____
  (Includes all items pictured on previous page.)

Other Books

_____   ____ copies X _____   = $ _____

_____   ____ copies X _____   = $ _____

_____   ____ copies X _____   = $ _____

_____   ____ copies X _____   = $ _____

                                    Shipping & Handling $ _____

                                    Subtotal $ _____

                                    Sales Tax (8.25%-TX Only) $ _____

                                    Total (U.S. Dollars Only) $ _____

Shipping and Handling Charges

Total $ Amount	Up to $49	$50-$99	$100-$249	$250-$1199	$1200-$2999	$3000+
Charge	$7	$9	$16	$30	$80	$125

Name _____ Job Title _____

Organization _____ Phone _____

Shipping Address _____ Fax _____

Billing Address _____ E-mail _____
                                         (required for PowerPoint Presentation.)
City _____ State _____ ZIP _____

❑ Please invoice (Orders over $200) Purchase Order Number (if applicable) _____

Charge Your Order: ❑ MasterCard   ❑ Visa   ❑ American Express

Credit Card Number _____ Exp. Date _____

Signature _____

❑ Check Enclosed (Payable to: CornerStone Leadership)

Fax	**Mail**	**Phone**
972.274.2884	P.O. Box 764087	888.789.5323
	Dallas, TX 75376	

www.**CornerStoneLeadership**.com

CornerStone Leadership is committed to providing new
and enlightening products to organizations worldwide.
Our mission is to fuel knowledge with practical resources
that will accelerate your team's productivity,
success and job satisfaction!

CornerStone
Leadership Institute

www.CornerStoneLeadership.com

*Start a crusade in your organization –
have the courage to learn, the vision to lead,
and the passion to share.*